THOUGHTS
FROM A GARDEN SEAT

VOLUME 2

Thoughts
From a Garden Seat

VOLUME 2

by
Derek Turton

Published by Derek Turton
158, Sancroft Road,
Spondon,
Derby,
DE21 7LD

British Library Cataloguing-in-Publication data
A catalogue record for this book is available from the British Library

ISBN 978-1-8381893-1-0

Printed and bound by Jellyfish Solutions Ltd

This book is dedicated to the memory of Jean,
to all my family, and to my sisters Pam and Ann

Special thanks to Revd. Peter Dawson OBE
and Shirley, whose words of wisdom have kept me
on the right pathway.

Also to all who have been effected in any way
by the COVID Virus.

Contents

About this Book

In March 2020 the UK along with the rest of the world, was launched into the turmoil of the COVID pandemic. The effects of the Pandemic impacted in one way or another on everyone resulting in a time of stress and concern across communities.

In an attempt to cushion that impact, the author of this book wrote a series of reflections, some spiritual, some factual, some humorous, which were published in a book, *Thoughts from a Garden Seat*, Volume 1, as a compilation of these reflections.

This book, Volume 2 is a continuation of the reflections over the second six months of the COVID crisis. The thoughts and memories stimulated by the reflections have proved to be a lifeline to many who have been isolated or housebound as a result of the national restrictions. It has also proved to be a gateway to Bible Study and understanding of some of the scriptures.

This book will continue to stir the memories of the past, challenge our priorities of the present, guide a pathway to the future through the scriptures and give hope and assurance through our Lord Jesus Christ.

About the Author

Derek Turton was born in 1948 and is a born and bred Yorkshireman, originating from the northern town of Bradford and his experiences of life in the 1960s will strike a chord with many readers of that era. After leaving school at 15 he worked as an apprentice bricklayer in his father's building business but left to enter Local Government in 1969, a career that would last over 40 years. Derek migrated south to Derby in 1973 and still lives in a suburb of the City.

His experiences as a Fellow of the Royal Institute of Chartered Surveyors, a Justice of the Peace (both now retired) and an active accredited Local Preacher have provided him with an insight into many sides of life some of which are reflected in this book.

Derek's wife Jean, died in 2012, and he has been well supported by his three daughters, seven grandchildren and great granddaughter,

After his family, Derek has a passion for vintage farm tractors and classic cars and can often be seen driving one of them along the country lanes of Derbyshire or at many of the rallies held in the area.

This is his second book, the first being Volume 1, which proved to be extremely popular and Volume 2 is a product of the demand from readers.

Foreword

Revd. Peter Dawson OBE

The second volume of Derek Turton's reflective thoughts from his garden seat is as compellingly readable as the first. His developing style now takes him into the territory where distinguished authors live.

In his new book each of the thirty pieces deals with a different situation in everyday life and cleverly relates to a passage of scripture. Often the material is autobiographical, which adds to its impact, not least when it relates to the effect of the coronavirus on people's lives.

Derek Turton writes with great skill, his words laced with wisdom to make you think and humour to make you laugh. Sometimes, like all thoughtful observers of life, he laughs at himself.

This book is for what the Prayer Book calls all sorts of conditions of people. Every practicing Christian, and anyone on the journey to truth, should read this book. It could save your life.

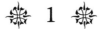

1

Bill Brown

Matthew, Mark, Luke and John

Bill Brown sat at his desk in the Post Section of United Insurance Ltd. It was exactly 9.00am and he had followed the same routine as he had done on the average day for the past 30 years.

His fingers played with the edges of the letter that lay in front of him on the desk. It was a letter that he had extracted from a plain brown envelope. The envelope was not there when he left the office on the previous evening, but was there this morning when he arrived.

There was a name typed on the front of the envelope and it read, 'Mr. B. Brown (Post Section)'.

Bill Brown was a Bill, not a William. His birth certificate read; *First name* – Bill.
Christian name – Brown. *Father's name* – Bill Brown.
Mother's name – Mary Brown.

Bill's grandfather was Bill Brown and so was his father, in fact all first born sons of the Brown dynasty were Bill.

No one could describe Bill as being exceptional; he was the epitome of average. He never did anything wrong but paradoxically he did nothing that could be described as brilliant. His school report listed all subjects as average, and this was reflected in his exam results, average.

Leaving school at 15 years old, found him working as an office junior at United Insurance Ltd., where he remained all his working life.

He married Marjorie when he and she were 21 and they purchased a small three bedroomed semi-detached house in a suburban estate on the edge of Leeds, where they still live today. They have two children, a 17 year old son, Bill, and a 15 year old daughter, Susan.

Bill Brown could be described as an average man, in an average job, with an average family living in an average house, but this morning everything could change.

He had read the letter once and now read it again a second time to make sure he had read it correctly. It didn't change no matter how many times he read each word. The letter set out the terms of his redundancy very clearly and concisely.

At 5.00pm Bill turned his Ford Fiesta out of the car park and headed towards home although his mind was elsewhere. What would Marjorie say? How would the children react? What would he do with his life without United Insurance?

Marjorie was very sympathetic, saying, 'Don't worry dear. The money is good and I'm sure you will find something else'.

Bill junior smiled and said, 'Does that mean we can buy a BMW with the money?'

Susan, on the other hand was a little more constructive in her thoughts. 'We must find you something else to do', she advised.

Bill appreciated her enthusiasm but he had no experience of practically anything outside the Post Room of United Insurance.

Susan thought for a few minutes contemplating the skills and abilities at her father's disposal, then, in a burst of a Eureka moment she exclaimed, 'You can write a book'.

A frown crept across Bill Brown's forehead as he thought a book about what?

Susan was prepared for his response. 'You could write a book called, "The Average Man's Guide to Being Average in an Average World." It would be a best seller'.

There is a line in a song from the musical 'Jesus Christ Superstar' where the disciples sing, 'When we retire we can write a gospel and they will all talk about us when we are dead'.

They are reacting to Jesus explaining his destiny and his prophesised journey to the cross.

I don't believe that Tim Rice wrote these words disrespectfully, but using artistic licence to portray the disciple's realisation that Jesus was soon to leave them on their own. The events that would soon unfold before their eyes will be so life changing and crucial to God's creation that they must be written down for posterity.

Each Gospel is written in a different style suitable and relevant for a specific reading audience, Jews, Greeks, Gentiles and everyone.

The disciples knew that they had to reach out with the Good News of Jesus Christ, not just to a favoured few but to all people, the average person be they Jews, Greeks, Gentiles and everyone.

Let us not forget that the disciples were themselves average people, but through Jesus Christ they redefined the definition to everyone who has ears must hear.

Bill Brown wrote several books including; 'The Average Man's Guide to DIY', 'The Average Mans Guide to Home First Aid', and 'The Average Mans Guide to Making an Insurance Claim'.

All his books had average success and he sold an average number of copies.

2

Put Your Best Foot Forward

John 13 v 1–17

The COVID19 has without doubt affected everyone in one way or another, and will earn its place in the history books used to teach in schools in years to come. It is ironic that the saga of schools closing, national exams cancelled, and qualifications awarded purely on the basis of teacher assessments, will no doubt become the subject of many a Ph.D. Thesis in the future. Education is just one of many areas of our social structure that have seen unprecedented change over the last six months.

I'm sure that some of our young people considered the situation as having some appeal, perhaps an extended holiday, especially when mum and dad could have been at home also due to the crisis, and the weather was good. But for many it was a disappointing climax to three or four years of hard study. At the time of writing this Pause for Thought, one of my grandsons is waiting for an email message to tell him how his academic achievements have been assessed over the past year to give him his GCSE results. His future studies and possibly his career depend on that email. No pressure there then.

As a youth leader, some years ago I was involved in The Methodist Association of Youth Clubs (MAYC) and helped to organise Youth London Weekends, a time when likeminded young people came together from churches nationally and internationally. In one of the group sessions I asked what young people particularly enjoyed about school. The answer generally came in four parts; 1) morning break, 2) lunch time, 3) afternoon break, and 4) going home.

In my school days it would have been; morning play time, dinner time, afternoon play time and home time. How terminology has changed.

Actually my most enjoyable time at school was going on the school trips. These came along once in a school year and they were the highlight of the year for me.

One particular trip still stays in my mind after all these years, it was a fossil finding trip to Malham Cove in the Yorkshire Dales.

This milestone event took place in 1958 and the school informed all parents that suitable sturdy footwear was required, along with raincoats and a woolly jumper. The raincoat and jumper were not a problem but I think I only had one pair of shoes, worn for school during the week and polished up for Sunday. They were shoes but not the kind of suitable sturdy shoes for a fossil hunt to Malham Cove, and there was no way that mum and dad could go out and buy a pair of suitable sturdy shoes just for a school trip. So dad borrowed a pair of hobnailed boots from someone, just for me to wear on the school trip.

Hobnailed boots were really strong heavy leather boots with metal studs driven into the thick leather soles and heels. My boots were very grand and were obviously ex-army as they had been polished to a mirror finish, but unfortunately they were three sizes too big for this ten year old with small feet. Mum came to the rescue by supplying three pairs of dad's thick woollen Wellington boot socks that increased the size of my feet and did the trick.

The day of the trip arrived and with great excitement I crammed my feet, and three pairs of dad's socks, into the shiny hobnailed boots and clomped my way to school pretending to be a soldier on an army march. It was when I arrived at school that I immediately noticed that all the other members of the class were wearing pumps, sandals or light shoes, obviously suitable sturdy footwear meant different things to different people.

We climbed aboard the old bus that the school always hired for school trips, and it thrashed its way up the hills from Bradford through Keighley, Bingley, Skipton and on the narrow winding road to Malham where we disembarked. The teacher told us that we were going to walk to the top of Malham Cove and search for fossils and then walk back to the bus.

There are two routes to the top of Malham Cove, one an easy route that meanders up a grassy bank to the top, and one that was the more difficult route up a rocky escarpment to the top. Now hobnailed boots are very good on meandering grassy paths but hobnailed boots are rubbish at negotiating stony paths and wet slabs of Sandstone and Granit especially when the hobnailed boots are three sizes too big. Our teacher chose the difficult route up the Stony escarpment.

Those people wearing pumps, sandals and light shoes were dancing up the path like young Gazelles and Mountain Goats, but for me I was thrashing my way up the path like the old bus that had struggled to bring us here from school. It was a case of two steps forward and three steps sliding back. By the time I had reached the top there was no time for fossil hunting it was back to the bus for sandwiches.

I was not feeling enthusiastic about descending the Stony path back to Malham in my oversized hobnailed boots and was beginning to regret the kind gesture of dad's friend who had lent them to me. Then the teacher announced that due to the Stoney path being so dangerous they had decided to return by the meandering path down the grassy bank.

Now we are talking suitable sturdy footwear. Hobnailed boots rule ok.

I had to secretly smile as we boarded the bus in Malham and I saw the terrible state of the pumps, sandals, and light shoes and the state of the feet inside them. I looked down at my not so shiny, three sizes too big but dry and comfortable hobnailed boots and thought, 'Thank you dad's friend, whoever you are, nice boots'.

In the Bible when we read of the journeys made by Jesus and the disciples, they would have been made on foot. There were no made roads as we would recognise, they would have travelled on stony paths and grassy banks. The day time temperatures would have been quite hot and the atmosphere was dry so the paths were dry and dusty making it a dirty sweaty situation for their feet.

There was no hobnailed boots for Jesus and the disciples, suitable sturdy footwear in those times was sandals laced with lengths of leather string so after a day walking their feet would be dirty, dusty and unpleasant, and possibly this is part of the reason why ceremonious washing before a meal was so important in Jewish culture, not only washing hands but also arms legs and feet.

If you were a wealthy family you would have slaves or servants to wash your feet for you when you returned from walking, but even in the servants protocols there was a pecking order and foot washing was allocated to the lowest of the low, the job was so unpleasant.

That is the significance of Jesus washing the disciple's feet in John 13 v 1–17. Jesus the Son of God, the Messiah, lowered himself to be the servant who washes the feet of the disciples.

Through this act of love Jesus demonstrated that the highest rank in the structure of the Kingdom Heaven is that of a servant who is willing to give up all to wash the feet of those who are in need.

The message to the disciples was that they having had their feet washed by the almighty should not hesitate to wash the feet of others.

The Bible tells us that after washing all the disciple's feet Jesus returned to the table. In which case the Son of God washed the feet of him who would betray him, Judas who at that time had made up his mind to hand Jesus over to those who would send him to the cross. Jesus demonstrates that even those who are our enemies receive the love of God through Jesus Christ.

The disciples could not understand the spiritual significance of Jesus's actions and Peter initially refused to have his feet washed by his master. Shortly after Peter would deny three times that he even knew the man who washed his feet.

I actually liked those hobnailed boots, even though they were three sizes too big and needed three pairs of socks. They were different to all the other footwear worn by the rest of the class but hey never let me down and kept me warm dry and safe. I wanted to keep them but dad said they had to go back. He polished them back to their mirror shine with a bit of spit and polish.

3

Wash Day Blues

Acts 16 v 14   John 19 v 2

It is true that you can buy almost anything on the internet but recently I came across something that was for sale that I hadn't seen in many years. It was a Posser. For the benefit of younger readers, a Posser is best described as an upturned copper bowl attached to a wooden handle like a sweeping brush, and used as part of the laundry process before washing machines were invented.

As a very young lad in the mid-1950s it was my job every Monday to help mum do the washing by operating the Posser. The 'Peggy Tub' (we called it Peggy Tub but some called it a Dolly Tub) was brought out of the cellar and filled with hot water. Just for information, the Peggy Tub was a barrel shaped galvanised metal tub with ribbed sides, just used for washing. The clothes and bedding were added to the tub with some washing powder and I would push the Posser up and down to rid the clothes of all the dirt. Eventually mum would empty out both clothes and water from the tub, add cold water and rinse the clothes.

Now there is something else to remember, wooden washing tongs. Mum would lift out the clothes from the hot water with a pair of wooden washing tongs; big tongs bleached white through the washing process, with a metal strap at the end to make then spring back to the open position. She told me they were Crocodile jaws and would chase me round the room with them.

It was the next stage that always intrigued me, Mum would put all the white shirts and sheets, into the tub and then get a small white muslin bag containing a blue tablet and stir it round in the tub until the water turned blue. This was called a, 'Dolly Blue', but although the water was bright blue the shirts and sheets came out sparkling white. It was mum's little magic trick.

Life changed when mum and dad bought a Hoover single tub washing machine. This was powered by electricity and had a small propeller inside the tub which spun round to agitate the clothes. Unfortunately, it also tangled the clothes into one gigantic knot, the pyjama legs would be entangled with the shirt sleeves and bed sheets were a real problem. It took mum ages to untangle them all. It never happened with the Posser.

As time went on we progressed to a Hoover Twin tub machine that had both washing tub and spin dryer. After the washing process mum would lift the clothes out of one tub (with the tongs) and into the adjacent spin dryer. The whole machine would then vibrate so much that it danced around the room with mum sitting on to try to keep it still.

By this time the Peggy tub, Posser, Dolly Blue and me were all redundant. I was approaching teenage years so helping with the washing was not the done thing, but guess what still remained on the hook on the cellar wall; the tongs.

In Biblical times the colour blue or purple was significant. It represented sovereignty, power, wealth and authority. Royal robes were always purple to give a visual representation of the King or Queen's authority and power.

In Acts, Paul meets Lydia of Thyatira who was known as a merchant of purple cloth. She was a very important person in the community, dealing with royalty and the rich and famous of her time. She was wealthy and it is said she had two houses. She befriended Paul and his companions and after hearing him preach she gave herself to Christ. She is often referred to as being the first European Christian convert.

Some Christian denominations recognise Lydia of Thyatira as a saint particularly in the Catholic Church. Her Feast Day is the 3rd August, whereas in the Episcopal Church it is the 27th January.

Purple is also significant in the Temple, adorning the dwelling place of God. It was used in the carpets and curtains (veils) and in the garments of the High Priests.

When Jesus was being taken to the cross the soldiers platted a crown of thorns and put it on Jesus's head, then placed a purple robe over his shoulders, mocking the claim that Jesus was the King of the Jews. Little did they know that Jesus is not only the King of the Jews but is also the King of all creation.

Song writer Graham Kendrick (Make Way Music) invites us to, 'Come and see' – See the purple robe and crown of thorns he wears. Soldiers mock, rulers sneer, as he lifts the cruel cross. Lone and friendless now he climbs towards the hill.

I looked up 'Dolly Blue' to see what it was made of. Evidently it was made of blue dye and baking soda and manufactured by Reckitts – not magical at all, in fact quite boring, and do you know what? You can still buy it on the internet.

❈ 4 ❈

Yorkshire Belle

Luke 19 v 1–10

Childhood holidays tend to merge into one another and identifying specific years and the age I was at the time is often difficult. However, sometimes a particular event stands out and for whatever reason it presents a clear recollection even after many years. One such occurrence happened to me in the Yorkshire sea side resort of Bridlington.

In my younger days family holidays were always in a caravan in Bridlington or later on, in Morecombe, and I loved them. We usually went towards the end of August and there was always a vague promise of staying on after the intended week, into the Bank Holiday, but I never remember it ever coming to pass, dad always had to get back to work or some other reason always prevented it.

The particular holiday in question must have been in the mid 1950s; I would have been about six or seven years old. Every Bridlington holiday had to include a sailing trip on the Yorkshire Belle, a pleasure boat that I think still operates today (probably not due to

COVID). It was a large craft, bigger than a fishing boat and big enough to enable passengers to walk around and buy a cup of tea or an ice cream. There was even a man who walked around the deck playing an accordion to entertain the passengers during the hour or so cruise along the Yorkshire coast. On a sunny day it was idyllic as we glided across the water with just the rhythm of the engines throbbing away below decks accompanying the accordion. It was an experience that was repeated many times on subsequent holidays, but on this occasion it turned out to be different.

On disembarking from the Yorkshire Belle we ascended the steps from the harbour up onto the sea front, where usually we ran a gauntlet of photographers who pretended to take your picture, then getting you to pose for a proper picture that they would charge for, but on this occasion we were confronted by a stampede of people running down the footpath towards the amusement arcade.

While mum grabbed my arm in a steel like grip dad asked someone what was going on, had there been an accident, or was there some other emergency? A man replied, 'It's Lobby Ludd, he's been seen in the arcade'.

Now at the time Lobby Ludd meant absolutely nothing to me and it was considerably later in life that I learned that the local newspaper had resurrected a fictional character that if spotted in a seaside town, would pay out £50 to whoever identified him. Bearing in mind that at that time £50 was more than two month's wages for most people, all it needed was for someone to say that Lobby Ludd has been spotted in the arcade and the world and his wife would descend on the place armed with their copy of the newspaper to claim their prize.

In order to claim the prize you had to stop the suspected benefactor and say, 'You are Lobby Ludd and I claim my £50 prize'. Care was needed because it might be the wrong man and that could be very embarrassing.

I think dad could have been tempted to join in the hunt, but mum was not impressed, she couldn't get to the slot machines or her favourite Bingo stall.

I wonder what it was like on the road to Jerusalem when Jesus was travelling that way. There was so much noise and people running around that the Senior Tax Collector Zacchaeus couldn't do his work. After all it's difficult to concentrate on counting money when all that commotion going on, besides there might be something in it for him.

I can imagine him going outside and stopping someone to ask what's going on. Someone told him that it was Jesus of Nazareth who was coming and he would be passing right down the road where they were standing.

Zacchaeus had several problems, he was a tax collector so not well liked, he was in partnership with the Romans so that brought him enemies, he was well known for cheating people out of their money so that didn't make him popular, and to make matters worse he was unusually short in stature. There was no way that he would get even a glimpse of Jesus as he passed by, unless Zacchaeus found himself a vantage point. A high tree for example.

From his elevated position Zacchaeus had a clear view of Jesus and Jesus had a clear view of Zacchaeus. Jesus knew all about Zacchaeus and all his problems, but it didn't stop him talking to him, in fact it didn't stop him eating a meal with him in his house, in fact it didn't stop him from changing, and reforming, Zacchaeus.

Jesus said; 'Salvation has come to this house today for this man, The Son of Man came to seek and save the lost'.

Zacchaeus was a reformed character giving back the money he had gained illegally along with more of his fortune given to the poor. Jesus didn't give up on Zacchaeus, he changed him.

Just as Jesus will never give up on us.

Lobby Ludd became a bit of a joke with dad. Many years later when we worked together, if dad saw anyone running down the street he would often say, 'Aye up lad Lobby Ludd must be about' and if someone told him something that was obviously a lie, he would say, 'Aye and I'm Lobby Ludd but you don't get £50'.

I checked on the internet for the Yorkshire Belle, it is still in service but has been withdrawn for this year due to COVID.

❊ 5 ❊

The cupboard under the stairs

∼

an uphill climb

Psalm 95 v 1–7

Some of you may be aware that I have two sisters, Pam and Ann, both are older than me in fact they are considerably older than me, a fact that I remind them of each time we meet (aren't brothers wonderful).

Pam celebrated a significant birthday at the beginning of March 2020 and we managed to have a family celebration before any COVID restrictions were introduced. Ann is two years younger than Pam so I look forward to her celebrations after the restrictions have been lifted.

Both Pam and Ann moved from Yorkshire to Lincolnshire some years ago, Pam moved first and Ann followed two or three years later so they could be close at hand and take care of each other, important in a rural community.

Their local church is Horncastle Methodist Church and they kindly invite me to preach a couple of times a year. On these occasions my sisters and I use the opportunity to get together for lunch after the service.

Like everyone else they are enduring the social separation restrictions and because of their age they are considered vulnerable (as am I), so to make sure that they are both safe and well I telephoned them to check.

Thankfully, both are fine, Pam has resurrected her interests in card making and embroidery and Ann is further developing her skills in oil and watercolour painting.

In order to pass my time while staying at home, I decided to sort out the cupboard under the stairs.

In the process I came across one of Ann's oil paintings that she gave to me some years ago. I hasten to add that the painting was not in the cupboard through disrespect, it was removed from the bedroom/study wall during redecoration and I hadn't yet replaced it.

It's an interesting picture of Mount Everest in oils and I have to say that looking close up the subject is hardly recognisable. It resembles a series of blobs of thick paint dabbed on a canvas with a knife with not a paint brush in sight as you would expect. Then there are the colours, apparently unrelated blobs of red, green, and brown but not in a uniform pattern. Amongst the colours there are streaks of black and white which to my eye serve no apparent purpose.

Now I have to admit that I am not an artist. My attempts at drawing are best described as 'childlike', big bodies, small heads with sticks for arms and legs, so I admire Ann's vision skill and talent but close up I fail to recognise the significance of the individual parts of the picture.

But then, hang the picture on the wall and stand back to view and the picture is transformed into a majestic mountain rising up from the Himalayas, with a snow capped summit merging into a harmony of colours and textures. The black and white streaks turn into shadows and light, the reds turn into rocky escarpments, and the browns and greens turn into eroded weather beaten inclines. The picture comes alive and you can almost hear and feel the wind howling though the peaks. It is a masterpiece.

It's like our lives, there are times when we look close up and it appears to be nothing but dark skies and storms but when we stand back and view the full picture the storms fit into one small corner and the rest is bright and colourful and that's where God is, protecting, guiding and caring for us.

It reminds me of the present situation with COVID.

Looking close up it appears to be a disaster. A jumble of restrictions, financial uncertainty, illness, suffering and unfortunately for some death.

But if we stand back and view the complete picture we see, caring people and communities, dedicated NHS staff, coordinated efforts by industry to provide specialist equipment, innovative ideas and solutions to previously unknown situations and vaccines that will give hope for the future.

(Psalm 95 v 1)
Come let us praise the Lord
Let us sing for joy to God
Who protects us

O by the way – I am reframing the picture and it will be back on the wall before the end of next week. Thanks Ann.

❧ 6 ❧

Something to Get Your Teeth Into

Matthew 8 v 1–17   Mark 5 v 1–20
Luke 8 v 40–56

During the present COVID crisis, I have had concerns over several shortages on our supermarket shelves including that of toilet rolls and wallpaper adhesive. Well, I have now discovered that there is a shortage of even greater magnitude than that of wallpaper adhesive and possibly all the other items.

I received a telephone call from a friend to say that she had just purchased the very last 'Home Dental Repair Kit' from her local chemist.

It would appear that during the present crisis we are all embarking on a do it yourself culture that has no bounds. We have embarked on complex home decorating projects, and I have seen the results of home hairdressing and hair cutting (the good the bad and the ugly), but home dentistry had never come up on my radar until now. I started to think what other home surgery kits could be available, such as home broken leg repair kits, or home knee replacement kits (I'll have two of those please).

However, as there is no evidence of any of these items been on the shelves I can only assume that they have been stockpiled by panic buyers.

I asked my friend what the contents of the Home Dental Repair Kit contained. She described a large syringe containing an unknown substance which we assume to be filler, a scraping tool, assumed to be for cleaning the effected tooth, and some antiseptic which we assumed to be for cleaning the tooth before and after the surgery. I was surprised that the kit did not contain a mirror as it would be unlikely that the procedure could be carried out without the aid of one.

Now that would worry me, the mirror that is.

I have experience of attempting to trim a beard round the ears using a pair of scissors and a mirror and I can confirm that it is not an easy operation. The simple action of positioning the scissors up, down, left and right can be confusing to say the least, which combined with the contortion required to manipulate the hand to coordinate with the scissors, possibly explains why the artist Van Gogh had only one ear.

Apply this lack of dexterity to imitating dentistry fills me with fear and trepidation. What happens if the wrong tooth is chosen and the syringe of filler is discharged to no affect? There are no more repair kits available due to shortages caused by panic buying.

What is more is that my friend told me that the tooth requiring attention is at the back of their mouth, in which case should a bright torch have also been included in the kit?

I started thinking about how many, and what type of ailments Jesus healed during his ministry. I tried to list them – withered hands, paralysed legs, blindness, deafness, bleeding, Leprosy, mental illness (demons), unknown illness of the official's daughter, illness with Jarius's daughter, resurrection of the widows son, resurrection of Lazarus. But wait, we are told that the people brought all their sick out to Jesus and he healed them all so the list is endless.

He healed by touch, by prayer, by affirming their faith and in some instances he healed without any personal contact, and always when all human efforts had failed.

But his greatest act of healing was through his death on the cross and his resurrection on Easter morning. His sacrifice healed us of all our sin and through him we are now truly healed. This healing does not come from any home repair kit or not even from a doctor's surgery, it comes from the love of a God who so loved the world that he gave his only son so that we can live.

I haven't had the opportunity to telephone my friend since her call so I'm unaware of the outcome and if her home surgery has been successful.

In retrospect, I should have called her and told her

to look under the box to see if it said 'Warning – do not try this at home'.

While writing this reflection I have heard that Boris Johnson has been released from hospital and is recovering at home. I give thanks that God's healing touch has reached out to our Prime Minister and pray that many more people suffering from this virus will also healed.

After further research I am pleased to confirm that other home surgery kits are available including emergency replacement of crowns on teeth.

Best of luck with that one.

❈ 7 ❈

Home sweet
(temporary quiet) Home

Psalm 46

I must admit I love my house, I have lived here for 47 years and I can honestly say that I have never even thought about moving to anywhere else.

Finding the house was one of those predicted events. Both Jean and I knew when we turned into the road that this is where we wanted to live and when we saw the previous owner erecting a 'for sale' sign outside the house we had to stop and take a look. I think we said yes before we knew the price.

I had moved to Derby some four weeks earlier to take up a job with Derby City Council (not City at the time) leaving Jean and six month old daughter Sam back in Bradford. I managed to get a Council house as temporary accommodation so they could come and join me. We decided to take a tour around the area to see what properties were available and this house was the first we saw. We didn't look at any others.

We loved the house, the garden, the location and the access to Locko Park just a few minutes' walk away.

That was in May 1973 but due to the vendor's new house not being ready, we couldn't move in until November 1973. I think the vendor was worried that we would back out of the sale due to the long wait, so they periodically invited Jean to spend the day with them and they could introduce her to the neighbours and the shops etc. This meant that when we did move in we could hit the ground running so to speak.

At that time, although our houses were completed there was still some construction at either end of the road, so traffic passing through was fairly light. We saw plenty of horses, tractors, a green grocers van that came round selling vegetables, and would you believe it a mobile fish and chip van that came round on an evening.

As the years passed by the situation started to gradually change. They introduced a bus service so the road became a bus route. This was good as we could catch a bus from outside the house and be in Derby in minutes (this was before the A52 road works). Young families grew up and so what used to be a one car family became a two, or three or even four car family.

New housing developments around the village generated more passing traffic and the road changed from being quiet back water into a busy highway.

All these changes came to pass over a 45 year period so to a great extent they were imposed gradually and unnoticed. Consequently we became familiar with the rumble of the vehicles making their way up and down the road outside the front window.

Until the Coronavirus crisis.

Now we are confined to our homes and our cars to the drive or garage and so the traffic has greatly reduced.

I was sitting in my chair in the back garden, actually writing a Pause for Thought, when I suddenly noticed something different, it was quiet, not silent, but quiet, almost like it used to be when we first moved in. The birds were singing, the branches of the Palm tree were rustling in the breeze and somewhere there was a dog barking, but it was quiet. There was no traffic noise coming from the road at the front of the house.

It seemed a little eerie as though everyone had been abducted by aliens overnight, except me. I breathed a deep sigh and thought, wonderful, it's just as it should be, peace and quiet. Then I realised that it was wonderful because of all the wrong reasons. The situation was all wrong, even artificial, there should be traffic noise as its absence meant that people were not at work, not visiting shops, not visiting each other, not living their normal lives. The dichotomy of the situation is that they are doing what they have been told to do, stay home stay safe, and prevent the virus spreading.

So there I was, enjoying the peace and quiet but worrying about the peace and quiet, worrying about why it was peace and quiet and worrying about the ultimate cost of being peace and quiet. Why is life so complicated? It's definitely time for a coffee.

Psalm 46 says that 'God is with us', 'God is our shelter and strength always ready to help in times of trouble',

God is with us in the busyness of our daily lives, in the noise of the traffic going passed my window, and in the bustle of the supermarket, God is there in our celebrations and when we are worried and concerned and God is with us when we work together to overcome pandemics.

God is with us in the peace and quiet of my back garden.

I'm going to shatter the peace and quiet at 8.00pm tonight when I am going to clap and cheer and blow a whistle in my front doorway, for our NHS heroes.

8

Crop Circles?

Psalm 144

I am always intrigued as to how the human race developed over time, after all the stone age people had no books to refer to or any previous experience to help them learn or discover, so how did they live and develop?

For example, who first discovered how to harness fire and how did they do it? Was a matter of many burnt fingers until they got it right? Don't forget they had no matches, or firelighters and they would not know how to rub two sticks together because there were no boy scouts in those days. But we know from archaeological excavations that very early humans discovered how to control fire and use it to their advantage.

In addition to fire I wonder how early humans discovered how to grow, prepare and eat grain and cereals such as corn, wheat. barley etc. Once again from archaeological discoveries we have found evidence from early stone age settlements, of cooked food containing cereals which suggests that techniques of gathering grain and cooking it had been developed, so one of the earliest professions was the 'hunter/gatherer/farmer',

Evidence suggests that the early farmer had discovered techniques such as creating a furrow to sow the grain and early ploughing tools such as shaped branches and animal bones had been used for this purpose, sowing would have obviously been done by hand.

The use of animals as a power source is also a mystery, who was the first to even think to domesticate an Ox or even a horse to work for the farmer? But whoever did discovered a major breakthrough in early farming methods. I suppose it was the earliest environmentally friendly mechanisation, no pollution and lots of natural fertilisation of the soil in one stroke.

The industrial revolution had a significant impact on most industries in the late Edwardian and Victorian era, and adventures into steam power certainly changed the face of farming. Powerful steam engines were developed that enabled fields to be ploughed in half the time as with animals. Two steam engines working in unison across a large field would pull a large heavy plough between each other giving a straight uniform furrow. Steam was not environmentally friendly and carried with it undesirable side effects such as fire in dry summer conditions and immobility in wet conditions, and eventually it gave way to much more efficient, more controllable and affordable, petrol, paraffin and diesel engines. By the early 20th century companies such as Ford, International Harvester, and Fergusson were developing compact, powerful and manoeuvrable tractors that had multi use facilities.

Preparing the ground for crops is not straight forward and follows a number of essential stages. After harvesting the ground is ploughed, and this in itself is a science. Each furrow must be the correct depth, not penetrating through the topsoil into the poorer sub strata underneath, each furrow must be straight and uniform, and each furrow must turn the stubble of the previous crop underneath to encourage enrichment of the soil.

The richness of the soil is assessed and possible additives such as lime, fertilizers or manure (nitrates) added. Heavy chains or other specialist implements will them break down the tops of the furrows to aerate and the soil and gave a suitable tilth to allow the seed to be sown. Early tractors would complete each stage as separate operation whereas modern tractors can now plough the perfect furrow, chemically test the soil, apply the correct amount of fertilizer, plant the seed and roll the soil in one operation and with the help of satellite navigation the driver can sit and read a newspaper while it all happens.

Similarly at harvest time the old methods of scything the crop by hand now give way to complex combine harvesters that can automatically cut the stalk, separate the grain, bale the stalks and jettison the grain into a waiting tractor and trailer. Gone are the days of farming machinery being uncomplicated, robust, machines of a simple design. Now we have complex machines that are scientific, computerised and very expensive.

I own two vintage tractors both from a family of compact machines designed to be efficient and manoeuvrable to best suit smaller farms and fields where bigger tractors were cumbersome and unwieldy. My tractors are from the late 1950s but there are many machines from the 1930s and older that still appear at tractor and steam rallies. Their basic but functional design and construction means that they still function today just as well as they did when they were new (well sometimes and almost as good).

The well-known hymn, 'We plough the fields and scatter', is of German origin, written by a poet called Matthias Claudius. It was first published in 1782 and was based on Psalm 144 originally having 17 verses. Jane Montgomery Campbell translated the poem into English language in 1861 and added music to teach it to children in a London school where her father was the Rector. The harvest hymn became the most popular song from worship books.

The point of the hymn is to give thanks to God for the harvest but also acknowledge that it is God that gives life to the grain, also feeds and waters the grain, swells the grain through the winter snow and develops it to maturity through the summer sun and produces the harvested grain.

I attempted ploughing with my tractors on several occasions and I can assure you it is not as easy it looks. Just keeping a straight furrow is difficult, it appears fine when you are looking forwards but it is when you turn round and look behind that you see the true picture. On one occasion I was so bad that if I had kept on going I would have created a crop circle.

Now there must be a sermon in there somewhere, ploughing our own furrow but only seeing he true picture of our mistakes when looking back at the times we took our eye off Jesus Christ.

9

It's Harvest ~ Again

Psalm 67 Ecclesiastes 3 v 1–8

At the time of writing this we are at that time of year when we traditionally celebrate our Harvest Festivals, a time when our churches are adorned with large quantities of harvest produce, spread out in all its glory across the pulpit, window sills and festooned around the communion rail, and I love it.

Unfortunately this year, due to the COVID restrictions most of our churches look somewhat devoid of the usual seasonal displays and put together with the absence of singing voices, our thankful praise is more from the heart than from our eyes and lungs, but never the less I have conducted three harvest services in as many weeks.

Perhaps it is due to my interest in farm tractors and having a grandson who is a farmer, that I seem to receive regular request for harvest services but as I love the thanksgiving I relish each service. I love the smell of the produce, the different colours, and the abundance of the produce particularly the local vegetables and flowers brought in from someone's garden or allotment. In fact I love the whole concept of harvest thanksgiving.

I always think of a story in one of my 'Yorkshire' books. It is about a young Vicar who was appointed to his first, very rural parish. When harvest festival was approaching he was desperate to impress his worshippers, so he toured round his parish and visited all the farms requesting the farmers to contribute to the church's display and to attend the service.

On the day of the festival he was in the church early to help the parishioners set up the displays containing great volumes of carrots, turnips, corn stalks, platted bread, peas, beans, cabbages, in fact every kind of harvest produce you could think of. His visits to the farms had certainly paid dividends, the church looked and smelt magnificent and everyone was delighted.

It was all going really well until, the doors at the rear of the church opened and farmer Green drove three sheep down the aisle. He was closely followed by farmer Smith who drove his prize winning pig down the aisle being chased in hot pursuit by farmer Johnson driving three young heifer calves.

The sheep spotted the carrots and made a dash across the front of the church to reach them, while the prize winning pig made for the cabbages. The young heifers preferred the floral displays, so lovingly arranged by Mrs. Higgingbottom, who almost fainted to see her artistic creations being devoured by the bovine juveniles.

Just when our young Vicar thought it could not get any worse, farmer Jackson entered the arena by leading his giant horse through the West Chancel. The animal, which was usually placid, presented almost one ton of Clydesdale muscle and sinew that had a particular passion for turnips and had spotted the display from the first pew. Nothing was going to stop this giant beast from reaching his favourite lunch, and nothing did stop him. Chairs, tables, vases all went off in different directions while farmer Jackson hung on to the horse's reigns as if nothing was happening.

Finally everything settled down and even Mrs Higgingbottom had been consoled to enable the young Vicar to deliver his sermon on 'God's Gifts' and after a hearty rendition of, 'We Plough the Fields and Scatter' a successful evacuation of the church was achieved without further mishap. Everyone agreed it had been a great harvest celebration and there was an abundance of produce left to distribute to the needy in the parish.

As our young Vicar reflected on his sermon, it did cross his mind that he wished God had shared a gift of constipation on the various farm animals present as it took over six months to rid the church carpets of the smell.

Although I have never had any similar experience I have used my tractor on several occasions to illustrate harvest, which has caused great excitement among the younger members of the congregation (and one or two older members).

Harvest, after all is a celebration of God' gift of the culmination of the maturity of the crops through the growing season. As Ecclesiastes tells us there is a time for everything, sowing and reaping and the whole process is a gift from God.

But is harvest more than that?

H = Hope – hope for the future no matter how dark the situation is today we have hope and faith in our God and the harvest is a sign of his continuing love for each one of us.

A = Assurance – assurance that God is always with us and his wonder of creation will continue to give us life.

R = Resurrection – as the stalk is cut down it gives new life through the grain scattered for next year's crop, as Jesus Christ was cut down on the cross his resurrection gives us life everlasting.

V = Vastness – this reminds us of the vastness of God's creation not just the gifts of food but of all his grace and love that is poured out upon us every day of our lives.

E = Everlasting – God's love is everlasting and surrounds us for all time even in our storms of life he is there holding us above the waves.

S = Salvation – The Salvation we receive through our Lord Jesus Christ who died on the cross so that we can have forgiveness and be one with our God.

T = Trust – Trust in our God, Trust in our Lord Jesus Christ because he will be with us always until the end of time.

There is more to harvest than just the food on the table.

I once parked my tractor outside a church as part of a Scarecrow Festival. A family approached me requesting if their children could sit on the tractor to have their photograph taken to which I agreed. While the mobile phone camera was clicking the father said to me, 'How did you get the tractor here, on the back of a lorry?' I replied that it came under its own steam, to which he said, 'Does it actually work then?'

It's surprising how quickly you can go off someone.

✤ 10 ✤

Bonfire Night

Leviticus 19 v 18

Well Bonfire Night 2020 came and went like a damp squib, in fact if it hadn't been for one of my neighbours trying to demolish my greenhouse with a rather large rocket, I don't think that I would have noticed that this bizarre tradition had actually taken place.

A few years ago my granddaughter had a Swedish pen friend staying with her over the November period (do we still have pen friends?), She stayed with us throughout November consequently she had to experience our bonfire night extravaganza. We tend to forget that this festival is solely relevant to this country and totally alien to people from foreign lands. This was the case with Mona (the pen friend from Sweden) so we had to try and explain why we not only set fire to piles of wood, polluting the atmosphere for a couple days, but we also make effigies of a historical terrorist and burn them as well. Add to this the fact that we then buy explosives and attempt to blow our gardens (or our neighbour's gardens), to bits and it's not surprising it is difficult for our continental friend to grasp the reasoning. I suspect that they do similar weird events in Sweden.

Although today's bonfire celebrations have become rather grand affairs similar events in the late 1950s were equally as exciting to this 12 year old lad at the time.

Bonfire night actually started about two weeks before November 5th because that was the time that we started, 'chumping'. Now 'chumping', involved scouring the neighbourhood for bonfire material. It meant going out after school and on Saturdays collecting anything that people didn't want anymore and were willing to donate it to the bonfire to be burnt. This could be tree pruning, old fences and other wooden items, but also included settees, chairs and even mattresses. Environmental pollution didn't come into it in those days. All the bonfire fodder was collected and stored in our back yards, and in our case, covered with an old tarpaulin off the back of old army truck.

The road at the front of our terrace houses was unmade and at one point just past our house it became quite wide, so this was the perfect spot to build our communal bonfire. All the dads would build the bonfire the night before and someone would have the responsibility of lighting it when it started to get dark on the night. There was always an issue as to who made the Guy Fawkes to go on the top of the fire. Some years we would half a dozen

Guys but it didn't seem to matter they all went up in flames.

In the eyes of a twelve year old lad the fire looked to be enormous and definitely bigger than last year, in fact it was the biggest we had ever done, until next year. As the fire became established the flames would leap into the night sky and sparks would fly in all directions. Mum would make sure that we stood a good distance away but all the dads seemed to be fire proof. I always wondered how the paint on the surrounding houses survived.

All the community from the terrace would take part in one way or another either chumping, fire building or providing food on the night. Someone would bring out some cups of soup, usually tomato; someone else would bring out a plate of parkin (a Yorkshire version of sticky gingerbread), someone else would make toffee apples and bonfire toffee, and it would be shared around while we stood at a safe distance from the fire. The fish and chip shop on the end of the terrace did a great trade.

All the houses had a low stone wall to the front garden, at one time they had iron railings but they disappeared in the war effort, but what was left was a perfect stage for fireworks. As every house had their own display it looked resplendent, not big bang but more sparkle and fizz. The big bangs tended to appear later in the night when the older young people were still round the fire and we were indoors.

Bonfire or Guy Fawkes' night is a British tradition with its roots in a historical event. The Bible also has festivals and celebrations which similarly have roots in tradition.

There are many festivals in the Jewish calendar that are very important to the Jews both historically and today. Not only do they allow for communities to gather together but they also link Jews to their past and the origin of their race.

Many of the festivals come from the word of God and can be found in the book of Leviticus, which contains the regulations for worship and religious ceremonies of the Jewish people in ancient Israel.

Jesus uses some of the words from Leviticus to explain the second new covenant that he brought to the world. Leviticus 19 v 18 says love your neighbour as you love yourself and Jesus added this to Love the Lord your God with all your heart and with all your soul and love your neighbour as you love yourself.

A few years ago I went back to Bradford and while I was there I visited my old house on Glendare Terrace. It was still there and looked highly desirable. But the road to the front of the house had been made up and now was tarmac. Where does the bonfire go now?

❊ 11 ❊

When I was a Lad at School

Matthew 4 v 23–25

During the COVID pandemic arguably the most controversial aspect has been the education system and the disruption to our schools. My daughter, who is a teacher, was explaining to me her new role of teaching on line using her lap top and the internet rather than the classroom. While we were talking my grandson was addressing complicated mathematical equations on his lap top as part of his school on line studies.

I started to think about my recollections of school life in the late 1950s. My lap top at that time was a chalk board which was kept in a box by the classroom door (no health and safety considerations, anyone by the chalk board box was in danger of being battered by the door). Next to the chalk boards was a biscuit tin full of white chalk sticks which we used to copy the letters of the alphabet, written by the teacher, from the blackboard at the front of the class. When we had filled our chalk board with letters we would clean it with the sleeve of our jumper or leg of our short trousers, and we would start again. At the end of the lesson the chalk board monitor would collect the boards from everyone and put them back in the box, dodging the door.

That brings me onto another point, who decided who the classroom monitors would be? It was always the same people but never me. Every time a monitor was required we went through the same procedure, the teacher would say. 'We want two strong boys to carry the milk crate, two to give out the bottles, and two to give out the straws'. I think the selection process was unfair as no matter how hard I thrust my arm into the air I was never picked. The two boys would bring the milk crate into the classroom and place it in front of the radiator, two other people would hand out the bottles and two more would hand out the straws (who know where the fingers had been before handling the straws). All this gave the school milk its particular school milk flavour similar to wall paper paste.

There was a multitude of class monitor jobs, pencil monitor, book monitor, milk monitor, but the favourite job was undoubtedly the bell monitor. This person had the job of ringing the bell at playtime, and it was always a girl, never me. This obviously left me with a complex for the rest of my life against bell ringing.

Sometimes we had a visit from the school nurse and we all had to que up in the hall and file past her while she rummaged through our hair, looked in our ears and at our finger nails. The school nurse always had a funny look on her face as if she had encountered a bad smell.

Play time was good and we could run around and let off steam. It was a favourite to fasten the top button of our coat under our chin and let it flow out behind as a cloak. This immediately transformed us into The Lone Ranger or Rob Roy or whoever was the hero of the day.

Some of the older boys would bring something into school from home and start a 'craze' and everyone would want one like it. One such craze was a whip and top but the teacher eventually confiscated them as they were too dangerous even with the relaxed attitude to health and safety. The next day the same boy brought in a magnifying glass and started to melt the paint on the school fence using the rays of the sun. The teacher confiscated the magnifying glass as well.

We did have Conker competitions in autumn and there were many scientific ways of treating your conker to make a winner over all the others. Marinating it in vinegar was a favourite or baking it in the oven, but none seemed to be effective.

I always found it strange that at the end of the day, before we could go home, we had to lift up our chairs and place them on top of our desk. Any other part of the day this would have been a criminal offence but at the end of the day it was permitted. It never entered my head that it could be to help the cleaner who came into school when we had gone home. I thought it was some ritual like saying a prayer and singing a children's hymn to mark the start and end of the day.

In Paul's letters to the churches in Rome and Corinth he stresses the importance of learning from the Gospels and emphasises to the believers that their faith cannot be strong without the knowledge and wisdom attained from the teaching of Jesus Christ. There is no better source of Jesus's teaching than in the Gospel of Matthew.

Matthew was a Jew writing for the Jews explaining Jesus's teaching on a way of life that will be righteous in the eyes of God. These include the Beatitudes, teaching about the Law, teaching about anger, adultery, divorce, vows, revenge, love, charity, prayer, riches in Heaven and possessions.

Most important are Jesus's teaching of salvation and the Good News of everlasting life in the Kingdom of Heaven.

No wonder Paul puts so much emphasis on the need to learn through the Gospel.

The great thing about school was that you mixed with all sorts of characters, some who were a good influence and some who were not so good. It is part of the growing up process to separate the two extremes and feed from the positive while rejecting the negative.

One thing that is certain that learning is not a process that is just for schools, it is a process that continues throughout life.

12

Press Button B
and Get Your Money Back

Genesis 41 v 25–34   Luke 2 v 1

I read a newspaper article recently about me. It is a strange experience reading what someone else has compiled about you; I read it to see if there was anything there that I didn't know about myself. The pivotal point of the article was that I had produced my first book at the age of 72 (actually I was aware of that fact) and why I hadn't done it before. The newspaper reporter had interviewed me over the telephone due to not being able to visit because of COVID restrictions, and as we talked I thought of how the conversation would have been different back in the 1950s.

I can remember the first telephone that was installed in our house. My dad needed one for his building business and after much deliberation mum finally agreed. The telephone was black Bakelite with a bright silver metal dial with finger holes corresponding to numbers from 0 to 9. We were on a shared line which meant that the telephone line outside the house served both our house and the house across the road. It was cheaper to install this way as opposed to a dedicated line, but it did mean that only one user could make calls at one time and It also meant that we could listen in to their conversations and vice versa.

Making calls was also different, we could only dial a local call, but any other calls that were long distance (trunk calls), had to be through the operator. This was achieved by dialing 0 and requesting the number, but we could only do this after 6.00pm because it was cheaper at that time.

Of course there were no mobile phones or cordless phones and I can recall that our telephone had a cord that had a life of its own. It used to twist and curl up effectively making it shorter in length resulting in the phone being regularly pulled off the table.

All telephone calls were paid for by the minute, local calls being cheaper than trunk calls (which were cheaper after 6.00pm). Mum and dad were fanatical about the cost of the calls and they installed a wooden box next to the phone to put money in after every call. I was far too young to be allowed to use the phone but my sisters used to spent hours on the phone (according to mum and dad) and they had to put money in the box.

If you did not have a telephone at home, you could use the telephone box which to me as a lad was great fun. You had to follow a strict procedure in order to make a call. First you had to remember the number to be dialled, then the receiver could be lifted and the correct money inserted into the slot. Now you could dial the number. If the call was answered, then the button marked A must be pressed and then you could speak. If the call was not answered you had to press the button marked B and the money was returned. As a very young lad, every time I saw a telephone box I would go and press button B to see if the was any money left in.

A telephone box was also a welcome shelter when caught in a shower of rain but you had to pretend to make a phone call.

There are many examples of how messages were sent and received in the Bible. Luke tells us that Emperor Augustus decreed that a census must be taken across the Roman Empire. With no telephone, internet, radio or any communications it would have been a matter of messengers sent out across land and sea to organise the census.

God's messages were sent through the prophets and their words of warning and repentance were spoken to the nations. Dreams and visions were also prominent. Joseph is well known for his gift of reading and interpreting dreams as in Genesis 41.

It could be argued that the most unusual message was delivered by mysterious appearing human hand writing on the plaster walls of King Belshazzar's Palace as described in Daniel 5. King Belshazzar had defiled the drinking cups stolen from the Temple. Somehow you just know that words on the wall written by a mysterious hand are not good news and it certainly was not good news for King Belshazzar.

The words spelt, Numbers, Weight and Division. His days were numbered, he had been weighed and found lacking, and his kingdom would be divided and scattered. All of Daniel's interpretation came to pass.

I can recall introducing the first mobile telephones into Nottingham City Council Building Control section in the mid-1990s. They were made by 'Motorola 'and were so big that you required a holster fastened round the waist in order to carry them.

A far cry to the slim mobiles/cameras of today.

13

The Train

John 20 v 19–26

I don't know about you but one thing I find can be a bit irritating is the advertisements on television. I appreciate that the considerable income generated from this kind of media, enables the programmes to be produced and broadcast, but even so some of the best efforts of the advertising moguls to persuade us of the miracles of their products, put together with the 'commercial' time allocated to them on our screens, seems to me to be a bit excessive.

When watching the commercial intrusion, I have started to play a little game of categorising the efforts of the advertising companies into: – 1) the confusing. 2) the humorous. 3) the insult our intelligence, and 4) the good.

1. The confusing are the ones that have two minutes of apparently unrelated images with usually a classical background music and leaves you with a feeling of, 'what was that all about?. A good test of the confusing is to turn the sound off and guess

the product; it's usually a perfume (very expensive one) with a French sounding name.

2. The humorous category is quite small due to the fact that on first viewing the advertisement is very funny, but after being fed the same message repeatedly at every commercial breaks the fun wears off. However, over the years there has been some exceptions, for example how many of you can still remember the PG Tips Chimpanzees, particularly the one with piano on my foot, or Lenard Rossiter and Joan Collins in the 1970s persuading us to drink Cinzano Bianco when most of it was spilt down the front of Joan Collins dress? Today the humour is still there but more subtle, as in talking cats and dogs, and aristocratic meerkats.

3. The insult to our intelligence examples are those that stretch our imagination to the limit, like pouring Blackcurrant juice, mud and oil down the front of a white shirt, dipping it into a water based solution and it comes out shining bright and not a stain in sight. There may well be an overlap into category 2 here. I did try the product. A white T Shirt with tractor engine oil poured down the front, dipped into the product and guess what – it came out black. There is a more concerning side to this category. Are we really expected to believe that everyone who takes part on a gambling site is going

to win a prize? I don't think so but some people do think they will. It's the power of advertising.

4. The good ones I like and I have used two or three in this category (I admit they are quite old now) as illustrations in my sermons. The football match in the trenches in 1916 is quite a powerful image for Remembrance Sunday, even though it promotes a super market. I have also used 'Simon the Ogre' (apologies to all Simons reading this), where a man is bad tempered at work, bad tempered driving his car, bad tempered at home with his wife and children, and bad tempered at the airport, but after diving into the hotel swimming pool he emerges totally transformed in fact he is Mr Wonderful, all due to the package holiday company. We can relate this to Baptism, the water symbolically washing away all the evil from us and leaving us different people, and if we change the water to the Holy Spirit, we are cleansed internally also.

The other 'theological' advertisement that I have used was called 'the train' and it featured, understandably, a train picking up little cartoon like passengers including a young couple with a pram, at the station. The train moves off and stops at the next station where the young couple alight and return with the child, now growing up, dressed in school uniform. The train moves off and stops at the next station where the couple alight and return with 'L' plates for learning to drive. The journey is repeated and at each station the couple alight and return with, a black gown and mortar board hat (university), wedding dress and finally a young couple with a pram, and it all starts again.

The advertisement is for a well-known bank who make the point that they (the bank) will be there at every stage of life to help support their customers and give financial support and security, and it is very comforting to be aware of that.

However financial security only relates to the material things in life, what about the Spiritual support that we all need at those same stations, no bank can offer that. In addition there is the obscure fact that banks make charges for their services, as my dad would say. 'There's no such thing as a free meal'.

Our Lord Jesus Christ is there beside us at every stage of our lives, even the dark times that are not planned for or expected, and all charges were paid in full when Jesus was lifted on that cross at Calvary. Jesus has been with us in the past, is here with us now and will be with us into the future, and that's more comforting than the bank.

Luke 20 v 19–26 Jesus said 'Pay to the Emperor what belongs to the Emperor and pay to God what belongs to God'.

14

Instant Success

Mark 7 v 31–end   Luke 7 v 11–15

I was in my local supermarket the other day. Visiting the shops is not something that I've been doing recently due to the COVID 19 crisis. At the start of the crisis my daughters and their respective families did my shopping for me and delivered everything I needed to my front door. As the restrictions continued I was introduced to on-line shopping so the supermarket now delivers everything I need to my front door.

I have to admit that on one occasion I did treat myself to a take away meal which turned out to be quite an experience. Prior to COVID restrictions I sometimes frequented a rather nice Golf Club three or four miles away from my home. It is a place where you can really splash out on a special occasion in the upstairs restaurant or have an equally nice but more modestly priced meal downstairs. Like many such establishments the present crisis forced them down the take away meals route so I thought I would try them out and treat myself to an evening meal from their menu. I ordered the meal over the telephone and was given an appointed time for its delivery.

Now my previous experience of take away meals has been that the meal is delivered anytime, or sometime, by either a young lad on a moped or someone in jeans and T shirt driving a dishevelled Vauxhall Corsa that has been rescued from the scrap yard into the service of take away meals delivery, so I expected something of the same from the Golf Club. I couldn't have been more wrong.

To the minute of the appointed time an almost new Range Rover pulled up outside my house and out stepped a young man dressed in dark trousers, white shirt with a bow tie and a red waist coat. He carried with him a cardboard carrier bag with the club's name emblazoned on the side. Complying with COVD 19 guidelines he placed the bag on my door step and stepped back and conversed with me from two metres. He asked if I required anything else, a bottle of wine perhaps. I looked round to make sure I was at home and transported to their restaurant, but answered that I did not require anything else. The young man wished me, 'enjoy your meal' and drove off in his Range Rover. I was unsure if I should go and change into my suit and get out the best knife and fork and plates only used for special occasions, before I could eat my meal.

But that was then and now I'm back to earth with a bump in my local Coop.

Surprisingly I have missed the experience of selecting the items that I require off the shelves. There is something about selecting the specific tin, packet, tray of meat or item of vegetables that is somehow satisfying, so armed with my face covering and subjecting my hands to the sanitizer spray at the entrance and keeping to the 2m distancing marking on the floor, I entered my local Coop. My intension was to prepare a spaghetti bolognaise so I was searching for the ingredients when I noticed in the freezer cabinet a spaghetti bolognaise meal for one, a meal made in an instant.

I was intrigued, it takes me 45 minutes to prepare my version and yet this was a meal ready in an instant, how do they do it.

Reading the label it transpires that the meal takes 4 minutes in the microwave oven and a further 1 minute to rest before eating. I thought that is not instant, it takes at least five minutes.

Across the aisle I noticed the selection of coffees, one of which was 'instant coffee'. My coffee machine takes about fifteen minutes and even using granules I have to boil the kettle; again it's not actually 'instant'. So what do we actually mean by 'instant'?

At one time it was thought light was instant and what our eyes saw was happening instantaneously, but then Albert Einstein discovered that light travelled at a certain speed so consequently, by the time an activity had taken place and travelled to our eyes and had been received and had been processed by our brain, time had elapsed so it could not have been instantaneous. (I hope you're keeping up with this because it's educational).

However, in the Bible we find many references to Jesus instantly changing people's lives, particularly in relation to healing and miracles.

When Jesus was at the wedding at Cana (John 2) the water was changed into the best wine in an instant in fact even the servants carrying the jars never saw it happening until they poured it out.

In Mark 5 v 21 we read of a woman who had been suffering for many years despite the best efforts of her doctor and physician, but when she touched the edge of Jesus's cloak she was healed instantly.

Similarly, when Jesus healed the deaf mute in Mark 7 v 31, the man's hearing and speech returned instantly. Perhaps his spiritual hearing and his ability to shout and praise God also returned instantly.

All the miracles that Jesus performed defy human logic, but none so much as the raising to life of Lazarus in John 11 v 43, and the raising to life of the widow's son in Luke 7 v 11. Both these men returned to life from death instantly after a command from Jesus. As it has been said many times in human terms it is impossible but everything and anything is possible through God and his Son our Lord Jesus Christ.

But for Jesus relief from the suffering on the cross was not instant and he would have felt the pain of the nails, the crown of thorns and the spear in his side before he returned to the Father.

For us, through Jesus's death and resurrection, our sins have been forgiven instantly and through faith we can be one with God and look forward to everlasting life in the Kingdom of Heaven.

I found all the ingredients for my Spaghetti Bolognaise but on returning home I discovered I had no spaghetti. I had Cottage Pie instead which was equally as nice – not as nice as the Golf Club take away though.

✤ 15 ✤

Come on Light my Fire

Daniel 3 v 19–25

In 1990 I became Head of Building Control at Nottingham City Council, a post I held for twenty years. I led a team who were responsible for all matters relating to Building Regulations and associated legislation across the City.

The regulations were complex and wide reaching covering all aspects of building design and construction in all types of buildings be it a garage in the back garden to a multi storey office block. The regulations were divided into various sections each section dealing with a particular aspect of construction and design and one section dealt with Fire Precautions and Means of Escape. Obviously with issues relating to fire there had to be close liaison with the Fire Service which resulted in regular meetings with the Fire Officer in order to maintain a coordinated approach to fire safety.

It was at one such meeting in 1999 when I was discussing fire safety in domestic dwellings with the Fire Officer at Bestwood Lodge Fire HQ on the outskirts of Nottingham. There was concern over an increase in incidents in dwellings on a national scale and we were looking for possible solutions that could be adopted to address the problem. One solution that was suggested was the installation of domestic sprinkler systems.

Sprinklers are small water jets that automatically activate when fire is detected and although they are widely used in industrial buildings were not common in dwellings.

The discussion revolved around how we could determine the effectiveness of domestic sprinklers and the answer was to set fire to someone's house but that would only give us half the answer. What we should really do was to set fire to two people's houses one with sprinklers and one without, and assess the difference. There was one flaw in our plan and that was we could not identify two house owners that would be willing to have their houses burnt to the ground, and as no one in the room would volunteer (no commitment), the conversation drew to a close.

It was a couple of months later that I received a telephone call from the Fire Officer, to say that someone had offered two houses that could be tested by setting them alight. There was a pair of identical houses in a row of terrace properties that were to be demolished for redevelopment. A specialist company had volunteered to set one house up with a sprinkler system and the other house would be left without a system. The two could then be compared.

This was an opportunity not to be missed so the financial aspects were all agreed and the test was scheduled early January 2000. Each house was furnished identically to give as far possible an accurate comparison, and fire appliances and crews were in attendance to use the exercise as an added opportunity for training purposes.

At the appointed time we all gathered at a safe distance and watched a fire fighter advance towards the buildings with a box of matches and a fire lighter (actually it was all done by an electrical igniter but it adds to the drama), and the buildings were set alight.

I had decided to take with me a stop watch and a new invention called a digital camera, to record the event.

In a matter of seconds the fire developed and in a matter of a minute the fire had spread throughout the ground floor. It took just three minutes for the fire to reach the bedrooms and within five minutes the fire was emerging from the roof and the entire house was an inferno.

In the sprinklered house the fire was extinguished almost immediately and never actually got a hold on the ground floor. Fire damage was minimal and water damage was restricted to the area around the source of the fire.

It was reasonable to assume from the test that lives would probably have been lost in the unsprinklered house but would probably have been saved in the sprinklered house.

I submitted a paper on the findings of the test to our representative Institute at the time which was published, and I also attended a meeting with the Fire Officer at the Department of the Environment in London to present our conclusions but nothing came from our discussions. The regulations were amended some time later to include the provision of smoke detectors but there was no further mention of sprinklers.

In the Bible we can read in Daniel where three people were saved from an inferno by God due to their faith and righteousness. Shadrach, Meshach and Abednego were righteous devout people living during the rule of the tyrannical King Nebuchadnezzar. They refused to abide by his order to bow down and worship false gods and forsake their beliefs in the almighty God. As a result the three men were condemned to death by being thrown into a fiery furnace, but not any old furnace, this one was built up to be seven times hotter than any other furnace, so hot that the guards who opened the furnace doors were burnt up by the heat.

Not only were Shadrach, Meshach and Abednego saved from the inferno, but not one hair on their heads was singed and their cloths had no smell of smoke.

Their faith and the apparition that he saw in the furnace changed the heart of Nebuchadnezzar and his belief in the one Supreme God.

Many of my reflections relating to my days of employment have to have a disclaimer that the legislation may have changed in the ten years since I retired but I am not aware of domestic sprinklers being introduced into new dwellings.

I have to admit it was very exciting to be involved in that experiment and I did keep the paper to the Institute just as a reminder.

Another Brick in the Wall

Genesis 11 v 1–9   Luke 14 v 2–3
Joshua 2 v 14–15

My next door neighbour is having extensive building work carried out to his house. Part of the work involves a two storey extension that abuts my drive; consequently, I have had a perfect view of all aspects of the work as it has progressed.

Having a heritage of building construction, including being a bricklayer myself in a past life, I find all aspects of construction fascinating so I have thoroughly enjoyed the past few weeks monitoring the progress of the work from foundations to roof.

There are so many theological and scriptural parallels interwoven in constructional practices.

If individual bricks are stacked one on top of another it is not long before the stack becomes unstable and falls over. However, if the bricks are interlocked, as in a dry stone wall, the structure is many times stronger. Include a mortar bed and joint and the wall is almost indestructible. If we try to work on our own we are limited in our achievements, if we work together in harmony with others we can achieve great things, if we enfold ourselves in the Holy Spirit and work together we can achieve anything.

As my neighbour's wall began to rise, it reached a point where the builder's legs were far too short, a problem that I experience often, and a scaffold was required to enable the work to continue. In an attempt to make the builder's life a little easier I gave my permission for the scaffold to be erected on my drive, so one day, very early in the morning, a team of scaffolding erectors arrived and erected their steel poles in a vertical, horizontal and diagonal formation that created a work of art compatible to any Renaissance sculpture or artistic work, towering high into the atmosphere, well, up to the uppermost point of the gable end.

Genesis 11 v 1–9, describes how the descendants of Noah built a City that had a tower so high that it reached into the heavens. It was made from bricks and tar and was an incredible achievement. I wonder what their scaffolding looked like. When God saw what they had achieved he thought they were too clever, so he mixed the languages that they spoke to make it more difficult, and scattered the nations across the world. That's why builders speak a different language to anyone else.

As my neighbour's scaffold and walls grew, so the work became more complicated, involving lintels over door and window openings, thermal insulation in the cavity walls floor joists and roof construction and much more. I began to realise that the financial costs of the work were increasing by the day and it made me think of Luke 14 v 24–30. Jesus was describing the cost of being a disciple and pointing out that no one should embark on a life with Christ without total commitment. No one should start to build a tower without first working out the cost or he may not be able to complete the work.

I hope my neighbour has worked out the cost. I'm sure he has.

The problem with a high scaffold is that it is a long way to climb to the top and difficult to carry materials such as bricks and mortar to enable the work to continue.

To overcome this problem the builder has installed an electrically powered hoist that can lift and lower materials in a plastic tub. Unfortunately he still has to climb the ladder but the heavy materials can be lifted by the hoist.

It reminded me of Joshua 2 v 14–15. Joshua sent two spies into the City of Jericho to collect inside information. While they were there they had to hide from the king's soldiers in a house owned by a woman called Rahab who enabled the spies to escape by lowering them down to the ground from a bedroom window in a basket attached to a rope. I can't help thinking it would have been a lot more difficult lowering two men in a basket at the end of a rope than it is for my builder using an electrically powered hoist.

In return for her help and assistance, Rahab was saved by God when the City of Jericho fell. She tied a red chord to the very window that the spies escaped from and she, and her family, was saved from destruction.

I asked my neighbour if the scaffolding would still be on my drive over the Christmas period and if so we could festoon festive lights on it and have a nativity scene underneath to compete with other illuminated gardens along our road.

Sadly he informed me that if all goes to plan the scaffold structure would be removed before Christmas.

Ah well, I will have to find some other source of excitement during the COVID restrictions.

All this goes to prove that no matter what we see around us every day of our lives, we can relate to the Bible and that God is with us in everything that we see.

17

All My Own Work

Genesis 6

Now that the evenings are getting much colder I have started lighting my log burner in the conservatory. It easily heats up both the conservatory and the dining room but also provides a fascinating focal point. Through the glass doors the flames can be seen dancing and leaping around the fire box and the colours change depending on the type of logs that are being burnt. Occasionally, if a piece of wood is slightly damp, it will crack and spit sending bright burning red embers ricocheting off the glass doors like a firework display. It reminds me of the coal fires that we had when I was young; we always had a fire guard in front of the grate to contain flying embers and stop them from reaching the hearth rug. This was obviously to prevent the rug from setting alight, but also because mum had actually made the rug.

She made several rugs around the house, some were plain, some were patterned and some had pictures emblazoned across them. Mum would buy a piece of hessian the size that she wanted, then cut up pieces of material into small strips and thread them through the holes between the weft and the warp of the hessian backing. The different colours of the strips of material made the pattern or picture on the finished rug. I think they called them, 'Peg Rugs'.

Looking back, mum was quite clever with her hands and I can remember her knitting and click clack sound of the needles when she got up to speed. I can also remember her and my sisters making dresses. They would buy patterns made of tissue paper and lay them on top of material over the kitchen table. Then they would cut the material to the shape of the pattern and stitch them together into a dress.

Dad was more my style, he made garages and petrol stations out of plywood and I would cover them with, 'Castrol' and 'Esso' stickers. He always made them just the right size for Dinky Toy cars and I had one for Christmas one year.

Dad and I also made a crystal set radio. Well I say Dad and me but I did little else but pass him a screw driver or pair of plyers. He made it in a blue metal biscuit tin box with a hole cut in the top to fit a dial which I turned to tune into a station. I regularly got told off by mum for listening to the radio through headphones under the bedclothes when I should have been asleep.

We did make a model aeroplane, it was a glider (no engine), made from Balsa wood. Each piece of the plane was pre-stamped into a sheet of Balsa wood and we had to push them out and stick them together with glue. The whole frame was them covered in tissue paper and painted with a liquid called Dope which dried hard. When it was finished I thought it looked great.

Dad and I carried it proudly across to some open fields close to where we lived and dad launched the aircraft into the wind from a high point to give it the best lift. Unfortunately these were the days before radio controls so when the plane left dad's hand it was on its own climbing high into the air on the breeze. Sadly everything that goes up must come down and we carried the broken bits of Balsa wood and tissue paper back home and it never flew again. Perhaps I should try again with modern technology.

I did, on my own, build a model boat, again from Balsa wood, with an electric engine run from a battery contained in the cabin with a roof that lifted off. It worked really well and dad took me to Lister Park paddling pool In Bradford to sail it. I wonder what happened to it (the boat not Lister Park paddling pool).

I also wonder how Noah must have felt when God told him to build a boat. The Bible doesn't tell us what Noah did before this commandment from God but it is likely he would have been a farmer but not at all connected with boats. His boat was no Balsa wood, pre-stamped, push out and stick together model, it was big and the only plans were the dimensions given by God which had to be specifically adhered to.

The enormity of the task just can't be imagined, not just the boat building but also reconciling the whole project with his wife, his sons and their wives. Putting up with the ridicule he would have received from his friends and neighbours. Then there were the animals, where did he get them from, how did he feed them?

Despite the seemingly impossible task before him, there is no indication in the Bible of Noah complaining, arguing or doubting God, in fact Genesis 6 v 21 tells us that Noah did everything that God commanded.

Perhaps there lies a message for us all in Noah's story. No matter how impossible the task that God presents us with appears, no matter how many stumbling blocks appear before us on the road, no matter how dark and stormy the future may appear, God can be trusted to see us through. We must do everything that God commands.

I have just looked up how much new model aircraft kits cost on the internet; Jet Fighter, remote controlled, all metal construction – £800.

I think I will stick to Balsa wood.

❀ 18 ❀

I Will, I Promise

Malachi 3 v 1

I am thankful that some basic survival skills for life were high on my parent's agenda when I was in my teenage years. The result of this meant that I am more than capable of cooking a decent meal, washing my own clothes and ironing my own shirts, capabilities that became even more relevant when my wife (Jean) died in 2012 and I found myself having to undertake all such tasks.

It was also fortunate that at the time the essential equipment such as washing machine, cooker and steam iron were all relatively new and have been performing well, until now.

This week I was happily destroying the creases in my best white shirt when my steam iron let out a loud bang accompanied by a bright blue flash and no longer steamed, in fact it no longer did anything. It was obvious that there was no chance that it would be raised again from the literal ashes, so I had to venture onto the internet to find a replacement.

I eventually chose what appeared to be a suitable appliance, not too flamboyant, no go faster stripes and no turbo power, and clicked on to the,' add to basket' icon. I was interested to see a message pop up on my screen explaining the, 'Company Promise'. I had obviously chosen well as this company promised to provide a quality product, with a quality service, and a quality delivery package including a guaranteed delivery date and time along with a free tracking service. What more could I ask for?

I clicked on the button that said accept everything including the 24 hour delivery slot and the free tracking service. Almost immediately I received an email message confirming the day and time that I could expect delivery of my new steam iron. I am impressed with this company promise.

The day and time for the delivery arrived, and passed, but no parcel materialised. I did receive a message that assured me that I will be delighted with my new purchase and would a like to comment on the efficiency of the service I had received.

Before I had chance to apply my fingers to my lap top keys in a suitable reply, I received a telephone call explaining that my parcel had mysteriously disappeared and was no longer on the delivery van that should have visited my house. What about the free tracking system could that help? The system seemed to suggest that my parcel was somewhere near Retford heading towards Lincoln.

After sincere and passionate apologies I was assured that my steam iron would be retrieved and delivered to my house the following day and would be none the worse for its impromptu adventure to Lincoln.

That's the problem with promises, they're so often broken.

Helen Steiner Rice wrote in her poem, 'The world is rife with promises that are fast and falsely spoken. For man in his deceptive way, knows his promise can be broken '.

In the Bible God's promise is a Covenant, which is more than just a promise, it is a commitment, an agreement between two parties never to be broken no matter what. God made a covenant with Sarah and Abraham that they would have children and through their faith in God they had many children even though it seemed impossible.

God made a covenant with the Hebrew people to lead them out of slavery and into a promised land and a new life. God kept his covenant but the Hebrew people failed in their promises. God both judged them and held out a hand of hope and redemption. The promise of the Messiah, the Redeemer, and Saviour was made by God through the prophet's centuries before the birth of Jesus but the Jewish nation were unwilling to accept him. Jeremiah 2: v 17 reminds the Jews that they brought God's punishment on themselves by forsaking their Lord and God. Isaiah 40 v 1–2 offered comfort to the Jewish people through a redeemer to be sent by God the Father, and Daniel 7 v 13–14 describes the coming of Jesus Christ in Daniel's vision.

Through Jesus Christ God made a new Covenant with all people that our sins are forgiven and through faith we can look forward to everlasting life in the Kingdom of Heaven. God has promised that he will always be with us and God's promise is never broken.

Well today is the promised day for the delivery of my steam iron. Its lunch time and I'm still waiting. However I have noticed that the cost of the iron has come out of my bank account, they are obviously more efficient at obtaining payment than delivering the goods.

There is still time I'm sure it will be here soon – promise.

19

The Best Laid Plans of Mice and Men

Luke 2 v 1–7

Robert Burns, the eminent Scottish poet wrote – 'The best laid schemes o mice and men gang aft agley,' He was writing a poem about a mouse at the time but his sentiment is as true as it can get. No matter how best we plan, our schemes are often thrown into chaos by the unexpected.

My wife Jean and I planned our move from Bradford to Derby in 1973 with meticulous precision, or so we thought. I had successfully negotiated the interview for the new job, Jean and I had visited Derby to look around the town and the surrounding area, we had even attracted a buyer for our house in Bradford and everything was going to plan.

The arrangement with my new employer was that temporary accommodation in the form of a local authority house would be available for six months when I commenced my duties. One week prior to my commencement we received a telephone call to say that the accommodation was not available.

We quickly made the journey to Derby and fortunately managed to secure a bed and breakfast accommodation in a house on Duffield Road, just outside the City Centre. For the next six weeks Jean lived at home in Bradford and I enjoyed bed and breakfast accommodation in Derby. Eventually all was well and we bought our own house where I still live today.

From the start we naively thought that it would be a simple process moving about 100 miles south from Bradford to the Midlands but we quickly realised that life is not that easy. The spoken word changes in that short distance and somethings have a different meaning which makes every day routines challenging. A visit to the bakers for example, I requested a selection of buns and was presented with rolls of bread. What I should have asked for was 'little cakes'. Spuds became potatoes and an alley between houses changed from a snicket into a ginnel.

Suddenly I grew feathers and became a 'duck' and on a visit to the next town of Ilkeston I became a 'youth'. In Bradford everyone was 'luv', a habit I had to get out of when working for a politically correct Local Authority.

I'm not sure what the local builders made of my Yorkshire accent, as words like 'so' and 'door' usually raised a laugh at my expense.

The views on gastronomic preferences also raised many eye brows. Someone described me as being 'strange' as we ate cheese with our Christmas cake and mince pies, and the fact that we ate our Yorkshire Puddings before the main course of our meal bordered on insanity.

Just when we thought that we were back on our plan, Jean and I discovered that we were having our second child. What did Robert Burns say about the best laid schemes of mice and men?

I bet Mary and Joseph and their respective families had everything planned for the marriage of their son and daughter. In those days marriage had two stages, betrothal and the wedding, each stage having its own ceremony and celebration. The Bible tells us that Mary and Joseph were betrothed so had gone through the first celebration and excitement was building towards the wedding.

It was at this stage when the plans started to go wrong. Mary was expecting a child and it took God's intervention to persuade Joseph to continue with the marriage. Then just when the new plan was in place, who could foretell that Herod would declare a census. Well actually the prophets of the Old Testament foretold it.

The journey to Bethlehem was not part of the plan, and not being able to find accommodation had not been thought out. Certainly giving birth to Jesus in a stable was never envisaged a few months earlier.

The chaos did not stop there, the shepherds visit was not on the agenda and neither was the subsequent evacuation to Egypt to keep the young child safe.

Mary and Joseph must have thought, 'What next?

No doubt Robert Burns was correct about the best laid schemes of mice and men, but perhaps we should look to the plans that God lays out for us all, those plans that never go array.

God's plan for Mary, Joseph and Jesus were written centuries before and we know that his plan led to our salvation through Jesus's death and resurrection.

I wonder if when our plans go wrong, it could be that God is making corrections on our behalf. Perhaps the direction of our planned journey would take us to the wrong place and God redirects us to where he wants us to be rather than where we think we would like to be.

20

The First Noel

Luke 2 v 1–5

I am reclining in my conservatory with the log burner blazing away listening to my radio. The newscaster is telling us of the slight relaxation to the COVID restrictions that will be introduced over the Christmas period. The radio announcer came on and proclaimed that it would be a different Christmas this year, not the usual festive experience that we are accustomed to. His statement left me a little puzzled because the festive experience has been a gradual change for me as years have gone by. Recent festive experiences are a far cry from those when I was 6 or 7 years old in the mid 1950s.

To ascertain just how different, I telephoned my two sisters (both are older than me), and had a long conversation with each of them about our recollections of Christmas past.

It would start when dad brought down the boxes of Christmas decorations from the loft. We had the same artificial Christmas tree for years. I think mum and dad bought it before any of the children were born and it was still being brought out in the 1960s.

The tree was a brown and green twisted wire sculpture with green paper pine needles and a red dot at the end of the branches. As the wire branches were folded up to go into storage, when they were unfolded the tree took on an irregular shape with its boughs pointing in different directions. The tree decorations were a little unusual, a toy car (a Jowett Javelin bought the year I was born), a battered and forlorn fairy on the top, and a selection of homemade paper lanterns and paper chains.

The room decorations were also ancient and came out every year. They were paper and folded up like a concertina then opened to span from the light in the centre of the room to the four corners. Some opened into a ball and they dangled down from the light.

Christmas dinner was always exciting and special. Dad had a secret admirer who, every year, left a turkey or capon (a large chicken) on our front doorstep. We never did discover who it was.

Dad would take it down to the cellar where it was cooler until mum could prepare it. My sister recalled that one year there was a commotion in the cellar because the bird was not dead and woke up to run round and make a fuss. It still appeared on the table on Christmas Day.

The turkeys were not dressed or oven ready prepared, they came complete with heads, feet and feathers. Mum would sit in the back room with a blanket on the floor and spend hours plucking the feathers off the bird and burning the stubble off with a candle. I don't believe that mum could cut the head and legs off so I assume dad must have done that.

Christmas Day was special and magical. We would all congregate on mum and dad's bed and have a sock and a pillow case. In the sock there would be an apple, an orange, some nuts and a sixpence (half a shilling or two and a half pence), and in the pillow case would be our presents, some bought and some home made by mum and dad. Any larger presents were left by Santa downstairs. I would charge downstairs to see if Santa had eaten the mince pie I left for him the night before and sure enough, only the crumbs remained.

We always had to have something new to wear on Christmas Day. My sisters had a new dress or skirt and blouse often made by mum and I would have new trousers or shirt. We had to look smart on Christmas Day even if we didn't go out anywhere.

Then dad would light a fire in the front room, possibly the only time a fire was lit in there, and the house would start to smell of cooking as mum prepared dinner which was always great. There was always great excitement when we got to the Christmas pudding. Who would get the sixpence wrapped in greaseproof paper hidden in the white sauce? I think we all got one.

The one thing that has never changed and will not change even with COVD restrictions is that Jesus Christ came into our world to save us from our sin and offer us everlasting life.

It is not important if the tree changes, or if the decorations festooned across the room are different, or if the illuminations in the garden are more or less extravagant than last year. It's not even important if the presents reach Santa via Amazon or the internet.

What is important is that the child born in the stable, into poverty, a King humbled from a palace into a manger, will grow into the saviour of the world. This is the good news that Christmas brings.

Perhaps next year we will be able to resume the festive experiences that we are accustomed but let's not forget that which never changes.

The turkey or Capon was delivered anonymously for about four or five years, then suddenly stopped. Perhaps the sender realised they had got the wrong address.

21

Don't Walk Under a Ladder

Psalm 25

My Mum was fanatically superstitious. I understand that she was quite ill after giving birth to me and certainly suffered from a nervous disposition for most of her life. She was a heavy smoker, something that undoubtedly was a major contributory factor in her relatively early death, but it was unquestionably a symptom of her nervous state and vulnerability.

All this culminated in a strange cocktail of traditional superstition and her personal made up variations.

Certainty a belief of bad luck when a black cat crossed her path was well known and not unusual along with not walking under ladders (although actually this is very good advice never mind superstition), but mum invented others that were a bit more obscure.

If, in the process of setting the table, two knives became crossed, they must be uncrossed immediately because crossed knives meant a battle was imminent. Similarly, mum would never stir anything with a knife, because to stir with a knife was to stir up strife.

The colour green was taboo and must be avoided at all costs. I once bought a green van and mum would not even sit in it never mind ride in it. Having anything green would only end in tears.

Items of clothing did not escape the superstitious shadow. If mum dropped a glove, someone else had to pick it up. If mum picked it up it was bad luck and spelt disaster, however, if someone else retrieved the glove then they would be the recipient of a nice surprise. If the glove was blue it had to come true.

I have to admit that if I drop a glove today I am delighted if someone else picks it up blue or any other colour.

On no account should anyone open an umbrella inside the house and if they did, it had to be held upside down (the umbrella not the person). I am not sure what the penalty for such an act would be, but mum wanted no part in it. Similarly it was woe and thrice woe on anyone who placed a pair of shoes (even if brand new), on the table.

Spilt salt had to be thrown over the left shoulder so as to blind the devil that was standing behind her, it was usually my dad.

How mum moved around the house also had relevance. She had to touch a particular chair, a specific place on the table and pick up a particular cup in a set order; otherwise her day would be a disaster. It was also tempting fate to enter the house by the back door and leave the house through the front door without first sitting down.

Then there was the piece of string.

The heating for the house and the cooking came from a type of Aga stove in the back room. Across the front of the stove was a handrail from where a piece of string dangled down.

The string appeared to be nondescript apart from a series of knots along its length similar to a Rosary and mum would sit in her chair next to the stove and play with the string in her fingers which seemed to help her relax. One morning we came downstairs to find that the string had disappeared without trace. No one would own up as to who the culprit was who had severed this piece of physiological well-being, but my brother in law always has a glint in his eye every time the subject is raised, even today. Fortunately mum found a new piece of string and the saga continued.

Psalm 25 has a message that assures us that all superstitions mean nothing and it has no relevance whether we open an umbrella indoors, wear a green jacket or drop a glove, because our protection comes from God. Whatever happens in this world we must put our trust in God and we will be protected, guided and God's love will be poured over us. His kindness and compassion will be with us as it always has been throughout all time (v 4–7)

We can turn to the Lord at all times for help and he will rescue us from all evil. We can ask for mercy and he will be merciful (v 15–17), we can ask for compassion and we will be relieved from loneliness and all our worries.

In these times of the COVID pandemic it is easy for us to become depressed and let the stress of the situation overcome our thoughts and lives, but God's words through the Psalmist ring true and give hope and strength to those who trust in God.

Although I do not share my mum's fear of superstition, I still walk very carefully along paved footpaths because we all know that if we tread in a nick we will marry a brick and a beetle will come to the wedding. ?????

✵ 22 ✵

Someone's Knocking at the Door

Revelation 3 v 20–22

After revealing my mother's infatuation with superstitions in a previous reflection, I now have to admit in indulging in a tradition that has been marinated in superstition for centuries.

Although I have, to the best of my knowledge, no connections with the highlands of Scotland, in fact I can recall only one brief venture over the northern most border on a tourist trip with Jean to Gretna Green, I have, for as long as I can remember celebrated Hogmanay.

This celebration which dates back to pre-Viking days is observed with great vigour in households across Scotland at New Year.

The revelry can last a week and involve such activities as, launching balls of burning straw into the air, burning replica Viking Long Ships, chasing an unfortunate volunteer dressed in an animal skin down the street while beating them with a stick, consuming large amounts of Whisky and partaking in the first footing ceremony.

It may, or may not, come as a surprise to learn that my involvement in Hogmanay is a very sober variation of the first footing element of the celebration both as a lad and as a responsible adult. For over fifty years Jean and I have celebrated Hogmanay with friends in York (with the exception of this year).

We always revel in good food and competitive games of Scrabble and Mahjong from where we are led into the lilting voice of Andy Stewart singing, 'Donald where's your trousers', and other Scottish masterpieces.

At the stroke of midnight the 'First Footing' ceremony is initiated.

First Footing is an essential element of the old year climax and the New Year welcome. Unless the ceremony is fulfilled precisely then who knows what bad luck will befall onto the New Year.

You can imagine how my mum would react to that.

First of all, before the midnight hour, someone has to go outside the house. This someone must be male, preferably tall, and dark haired. They must carry with them, a piece of coal, a pinch of salt, a piece of Christmas cake (other types of fruit cake are available), a silver coin and a dram of Whisky (or in our case Tonic Water or Shloer).

When the clock strikes twelve, the first footer is permitted to cross the threshold and re-enter the house bringing their gifts with them. They can then kiss the ladies and shake hands with the gentlemen before joining hands and singing,' Auld Lang Syne'. The revelry can then continue until retiring to bed at an earlier time than last year.

The first footing always reminds me of the Bible, Revelations 3 v 20–24, along with a painting by the pre-Raphaelite artist William Holman Hunt. The painting shows the figure of Jesus Christ holding a lantern and knocking on a closed door.

The door is overgrown and obviously has not been opened for many years. It has no handle on the outside so can only be opened from within.

The picture and the scripture represents each one of us, having Jesus Christ knocking on the door of our lives wishing to come in, but not all will open the door. Despite no response he never gives up and keeps knocking, asking for the door to be opened and his crossing the threshold into our lives. He brings with him not a piece of coal, or a piece of cake, or a silver coin, but light and peace and hope and love.

Jesus will not force his way in, he will not impose himself on the unresponsive. There is no handle on the outside to enable him to open it by himself. He must be invited from within. Verse 22 says, 'If you have ears then listen to what the spirit says'.

Let Jesus be the first footer over the threshold of your lives, respond to the knocking and open the door, allow him in and let him reside in your heart for all time.

First Footing does have its problems. I have always been short in stature and light haired so I have never had the responsibility of crossing the threshold. I have to say that considering the weather conditions at midnight in late December the first footer has to endure cold, rain, wind, and often frost and snow so I have never regretted my exclusion from performing this ritual.

A further problem is that as the years slip by it becomes more difficult finding a male member of our little group who has dark hair – or any hair for that matter.

23

Dear Sir 〜 or,
To Who it May Concern

Philemon Chapters 1–25

I received a letter recently, I know it's not unusual to receive a letter, I get them all the time, usually from Inland Revenue, Gas or Electric suppliers, and so on, but this letter was different. It was hand written, on lined paper and the hand writing was meticulous. It was everything that my letters are not.

I tend to type my letters due to the fact that my handwriting emulates an unknown foreign language and can only be interpreted by experts from Bletchley Park, but this letter was Copperplate Calligraphy. Furthermore, this letter was from someone who I have not seen or heard from for almost fifty years.

It was from someone who I worked with at Huddersfield from 1969 until I left for Derby in 1973. He had obtained a copy of one of my books from a mutual friend and on reading it had generated a multitude of memories that had enthused him to write to me.

There is something about a hand written letter that is special. Typed letters tend to be official and regimented, whereas hand written letters are more personal and somehow sincere. Letter writing is a unique way of sharing thoughts with someone else that is in a different location, and is increasingly becoming a lost art form with the development of email and texting. A letter can portray sadness, excitement, congratulations, a cry for help or a combination of all the emotions.

Experts tell us that a letter should contain six elements –

1) The senders address

2) The Date

3) A Salutation (greeting)

4) The Body of the message

5) Conclusion

6) Closing Signature.

The letter that I received contained all of these elements and all the emotions from events that had accrued over the 47 year period since we last met. As with us all it was a cauldron of good news, disasters, and at times suffering all laid out on the pages in a meticulous array of perfectly formed letters and words.

The Bible is full of letters, in fact it could be argued that The Bible is a consolidation of a multitude of letters written and handed down from generation to generation, some historical accounts of events, some reports of happenings, some of profound teaching, and some of prophesies and predictions.

It goes without saying that Paul's letters are significant and central to Christian Theology, but for me, one of his letters stands out as a portrayal of his tenderness and love not always demonstrated in his other letters. In this letter we find Paul acting as a mediator between a wealthy Christian convert called Philemon, and his slave called Onesimus. For some unknown reason Onesimus had run away from his master, an act that would result in severe punishment if he was caught. Paul writes in order to plead on behalf of Onesimus for clemency.

Paul's letter to Philemon comes from the apostle's heart and shows courtesy, tact, a little humour and love in order to get his plea on behalf of Onesimus, over in a tender but powerful way.

It has it all, dated about AD60 and written while Paul was under arrest, the letter has a passionate salutation and praise of Philemon's work and service in the name of Jesus Christ before launching into his appeal for Philemon's compassion, forgiveness and clemency towards Onesimus.

Paul was aware that to fulfil his request would be difficult for Philemon as it went against the rules on how to deal with a disruptive slave, but Paul points out that as Jesus forgave Philemon through Paul, so should Philemon forgive Onesimus in the name of Jesus.

In faith Paul is sending Onesimus back to Philemon possibly before an answer to his appeal has been received, he will return not just as a forgiven slave but as a brother in Christ.

> Paul's Epistle to Philemon has been described as, 'A true little masterpiece in the art of letter writing'. — Ernest Renan

> 'We are all the Lord's Onesimi' — Martin Luther

Unfortunately we have no record of the result of Paul's appeal but I have faith that Onesimus was received by Philemon as the prodigal son was received by his father.

I am just about to start my reply to my friend's letter, I tried hand writing it but reading it through even I didn't understand what I had written. I think to avoid him thinking that I have been taken over by aliens, I will have to type it, at least he will be able to read it.

24

From the Ashes of Disaster Grow the Roses of Success

Matthew 6 v 28–30

I picked up a leaflet recently; well it was more a booklet than a leaflet, published by the Derbyshire Wildlife Trust. It was dated summer 2020, and had obviously been written shortly after the first COVID lockdown had been relaxed.

I have to say that the information contained within the pages of the booklet was interesting and inspiring, describing the work of the Trust, their successes and their concerns for our natural environment and the state of our local wildlife.

One particular article caught my attention. It related to the state of the natural environment during the lockdown period. Prior to the COVID pandemic the threat to many of our wildlife species had been made painfully clear and scientists and naturalists have pointed the finger of blame on the lifestyle of all of us. However, although the crisis and the lockdown has for many been a traumatic and near disastrous experience, it would appear that in many ways the natural environment including our wildlife have thrived.

Lockdown forced us to stay at home, use our cars less, cycle more, and walk more and to stop flying to far off destinations. Believe it or not these changes have seen a measurable positive impact on our air quality and a reduction in atmospheric pollution.

Experts now tell us that due to lockdown, our air is fresher, fish have returned to many of our waterways, and birdsong is now louder and more vibrant (Jo Smith Derbyshire Wildlife Trust)

The imposed, 'stay at home' culture has resulted in other advantages for our wildlife, such as grass verges not being cut, and road side hedgerows being left to overgrow providing a much needed haven for small mammals and insects. A noticeable influx of natural wild flowers and fauna in the hedgerows has provided of explosion of colour along many of our country lanes and across our fields.

All this is good news for our natural environment but it is also proving to be good news for us. Evidence has shown that cycling and walking in the countryside is beneficial to our mental health in addition to our physical fitness. Walking around a lakeside or following a stream or watercourse is known to have a calming effect on our stress levels and even listening to birdsong has proved to help reduce the cares and concerns of everyday life. Those of us who are fortunate enough to have access to parkland or countryside locations will also have greater opportunities to observe wildlife species perhaps not usually seen.

I am blessed that I live adjacent to a large area of countryside and parkland, and I regularly take myself off to walk across the fields, stop for coffee at a local farm tea rooms (when COVID permits) and return home via a circular route. In recent weeks I have sighted Buzzards, Herons, ground and tree mammals, and the annual arrival and departure of the squadron of Canada Geese as they, in chevron formation, noisily pass over my house.

I can disclose that there have been many sermons mentally written while I have been immersed in the tranquillity of this alternative world.

The natural environment is an essential ingredient to the well-being of our physical and mental health, our spiritual fulfilment and our ability to cope with situations beyond our comprehension.

During this COVID crisis it is understandable that there are some people who are depressed and worried not just about the present situation but also about the future and it is natural that we concentrate on the negative aspects of the situation. However, the message we receive from Matthew 6 v 28–30 is clear, God will never desert us, never leave us on our own and will never reject us.

As God blankets the hedgerows with colour and beauty, and as he brings life back to the barren ground, so will he clothe us with so much more. We will emerge from the darkness of the COVID crises and we will feel the warmth of God's love poured over us.

From this crisis perhaps there will be a long lasting transformational change in our relationship with nature and through that change we will experience further the love and strength of our gracious God.

Many years ago when I worked in Nottingham, I sometimes used an underpass (now filled in), which tunnelled under Maid Marion Way. It was dark, unpleasant and often had a revolting smell. Half way along its length it crossed a second underpass and at the junction there was a small kiosk selling newspapers and soft drinks. Sometimes they also had a few cut flowers in metal containers outside for sale. It was a temporary haven in the middle of a dark unpleasant journey, an oasis of colour and hope.

Warning
Take care, if we return to business as usual at some point in time, will it spell the end of the wildlife revolution or will it start a new era of nature's rule?

25

Hello Duck

Genesis 8 v 6–12

We have experienced a few weeks of inclement weather recently, heavy rain and quite heavy snows, which has resulted in the ground being saturated. My front garden has standing water in the flower beds; however, the rear garden has suffered even worse.

I have 50 to 75 mm (2 to 3 inches) of standing water over the majority of my lawn and the path leading up to the dry stone wall that I built last summer.

I always fancied a swimming pool but not just like this one.

In the past I have had a number of welcome visitors into my garden including, hedgehogs, woodpeckers, pheasants, foxes, and on two occasion's buzzards from the local Country Park. However, the flooded terrain has attracted something that I have not seen before in my garden.

Two ducks.

It could be argued that ducks are not unusual but these two were white ducks, the kind that are often seen in farmyards and I suspect that their ability to fly great distances is limited.

When COVID permits, I regularly don my walking boots and walk across the fields at the rear of my house and visit Locko Park, a private country park with public access. The centre piece of the park is the large mansion house, Locko Hall, but for me the large lake is far more interesting, particularly the water fowl that either resides on or around the water, or visits seasonally.

I find that standing beneath a large Willow tree looking out across the lake and observing the life on the water unfold before me to be extremely spiritual. This has been the source and inspiration of many a sermon in the past. I can understand when experts tell us that walking in the countryside and particularly beside water can be beneficial to our mental wellbeing.

On my visits to the lake I have regularly spotted a multitude of species of water fowl all with their own characters, some of which reflect that of many human equivalents.

There is the grey heron who is the sergeant major, shoulders back, chest out, head up, standing to attention on the island in the middle of the lake. It must have a nest close by and stands guard like a soldier on guard duty. He keeps a close eye on the RAF Heavy Bomber Squadron that approach in formation from the fields at the rear of the hall.

These are the Canada Geese that come in low with their feet down like undercarriage, and then hit the water with a confusion of exploding spray that obliterates the birds for a second before they settle down. I can imagine a, 'Dam Buster' type of conversion passing between them as they approach; 'Red Leader calling, Target in view, right chaps I 'm going in.' and then the reply, 'Blue Leader – Roger Red Leader we're right behind you.'

All this excitement does not impress the mallard ducks; they are far too busy chatting up and trying to impress the girls. The boys have dressed up especially for the occasion, with their best suits on. Their colourful plumage with red, green and yellow makes them irresistible to the ladies, or so they think. They paddle around the girls showing off and dipping their heads in the water then shaking off the water droplets.

'Are you dancing?' Then the reply.

'Are you asking?'

Just like the Majestic Ballroom in Bradford on a Saturday night in the 1960s.

The crested grebe always impresses me. It has a stature and a design that is perfect for its survival. Its long pointed beak, slender sleek body, and an ability to hold its breath longer that any scuba diver gives it the advantage over other competitors for the food in the lake.

It could be the nuclear submarine of the lake.

When its sensitive radar detects food under the surface its brain cries out, 'Dive, dive, dive.' And it disappears in a flash beneath the waves with hardly a ripple on the surface, but where will it resurface? I scan the area of its disappearance through my binoculars but never predict the right place; it always resurfaces in another part of the lake.

Genesis 8 v 6–12

Noah had a dilemma, the water was receding and his boat had come to rest but as no other land was visible around him he knew he must be on a mountain top and not on low land.

How could he discover the extent of the land that was available? He sent out a Raven but Ravens live in high places and do not need low lands. The Raven never returned.

Noah sent out a Dove who feeds on the ground but it found no ground to feed on so it returned. After several further attempts the Dove discovered food only available at a low dry level, a young Olive branch. The dove now often represents a sign of peace after the turmoil, hope after disaster, and calm after the storm. Noah knew the flood was over and it was safe to disembark.

I opened my Patio doors and accidentally scared the white ducks off; however, they did not fly away.

Hello Duck

They just waddled off through a gap in the fence and disappeared into the undergrowth.

Ah well I will have to buy ducks eggs after all.

26

Hold it ~ What a Picture

John 2 v 1–10

A couple of weeks ago, observing the 12 days rule, I put Jesus back in the wardrobe. He was in his manger, wrapped in his own plastic bag and tenderly placed in his own individual socket in the polystyrene block that will be his home till next year.

Above him are a donkey and two sheep, and at either side stand Mary and Joseph.

It is a nativity scene that my daughters bought for my wife Jean some years ago and as it is quite fragile I keep it in the wardrobe rather than in the roof space along with all the other Christmas annuals.

In order to reach the nativity box's allocated space on the shelf, I had to move another dusty box which obviously had not been moved for some time.

Curiosity got the better of me, and I had to open it, after carefully clearing the dust from the top of the lid.

It was the photograph album of Jean and my wedding in 1969 and I could not resist the temptation to turn each page and view this slice of my history.

The photographs are all in black and white, I am sure it cost extra to have colour, and consist of the usual regimented poses for weddings at that time.

I was amazed as to how little I have changed.

With the exception of losing most of my hair and what is left has changed colour, growing a beard, more than doubling my body weight, appearing to have lost two or three inches (50 to 75mm) in height, and now having a multitude of facial lines around my eyes and across my forehead which are not apparent on the photograph, I don't seem to have changed at all.

Jean looks resplendent in a pencil style wedding dress and the bride's maids look equally glamorous in their coordinated dresses.

All the men are wearing Top Hat and Tails and look very smart, but unfortunately there was a problem when allocating the suits from Moss Bros. and some obviously went to the wrong people. This resulted in my suit being too big so the trousers and jacket sleeves could have been turned up several times, whereas one of the ushers suit was too small with trousers just below the knee and jacket sleeves at the elbow.

Despite this insignificant hitch, I recall that the whole day went extremely well. The sun shone and the weather was warm for May. Dad was happy after previously paying for two daughters weddings; he was relieved to have an easy ride with this one.

However there was one slight issue. Responsibility for arranging the wedding cars traditionally lay with the groom and Jean had a quiet word in my ear prior to the big day, giving me instructions that the cars must not be black, as black cars were for funerals. As I always follow instructions, I specifically requested, 'Wedding Cars' from the car hire company, stressing that I did not want, 'Funeral Cars'.

In my naivety, I was not aware that the difference between wedding and funeral cars came down to white seat covers and white ribbons. The cars were all black Rolls Royce.

I hoped that in the excitement of the day no one would notice.

I was wrong, but Jean and I were married for 43 years so she must have forgiven me.

There are many references to weddings in the Bible. The Old Testament refers to Israel being the Bride to the Kingdom of Heaven. Jesus used weddings and the wedding ceremony as illustrations to his teaching and preaching. In Mathew 25 we learn to be prepared using the wedding virgins with their lamps as an illustration.

The most recognisable use of a wedding in the scriptures is perhaps the wedding at Cana (John 2 v 1–10) where Jesus turned the water into wine. This is considered to be the first of the miracles that

Jesus performed and showed his compassion for the married couple.

It is interesting to note that the first miracle performed by Jesus was totally unnoticed by everyone except Mary Jesus's mother. The guests never realised that the wine had expired, the host never realised, the servants never realised the water had changed but everyone noticed that the quality of the wine was now the best it could be.

This is illustrative of the Wine of the Kingdom – saving the best till last.

In the box, in addition to the album, there are other memorabilia of the day including telegrams (do we still have telegrams at weddings?), copies of the table settings, invitations and a copy of a magazine called, 'The Bradford Bystander' (similar to Derbyshire Life), dated July 1969.

The magazine cost two shillings and six pence, and on the page for weddings there is a photograph of a couple called Mr. D. Turnton who married Miss G. Tintman.

Ah well you can't have everything.

By the way, did you know that, in 1969, you could buy a brand new Vauxhall Viva for £758.10s.6d. or a BMW for £2,197.15s.4d. it's all in the Bradford Bystander.

27

Family Tree

Matthew 1 v 1–17

I am still pondering over the photographs in my wedding album and as I thumb through the pages the realisation of the passage of time is beginning to have an impact.

Some of the wedding guests I have not seen in many years and one or two of the wedding party seem to have disappeared into the mists of time.

More alarmingly, one group picture made me realise that I am the only person who is still breathing. Still after over fifty years, I suppose that will be inevitable.

There is one photograph that seemed to answer a question that had avoided my comprehension for the past four or five years.

I am blessed to have seven grandchildren, five grandsons and two granddaughters. All of them look down on me, due to the fact that they are all taller than I am, in fact most of them exceed six feet (1.8m) in height. Two of them in particular have such height that they ought to have a red flashing light on their heads to warn low flying aircraft.

Strangely, Jean, me, and our daughters, are not tall people and we all struggle with high kitchen cupboards. So where has this lofty gene come from that has manifested itself in this generation?

It does have some advantages, however, when I need something retrieving from a high shelf I know who to call and it also means that they have to bow when entering my house which is very respectful.

For them it can be a problem. A standard size bed and bath is too short, which results in feet projecting out of the duvet or the bath water.

One picture from the album gave me a clue towards the answer to this conundrum. It is a picture of three generations of the Turton family tree, grandparents from my mother's side, my parents, me, and my grandparents from my father's side.

When I was a child we always referred to my mother's side as being, little Grandma and little Grandad as they were both vertically challenged, as was my mother. Little Grandma died some years before our wedding so only Little Grandad is on the picture.

On the other side was dad's parents, Big Grandma and Big Grandad, and there may be the answer to my problem.

Grandad Turton was enormous compared to everyone else. He stood head and shoulders above me, and waist, head and shoulders above my mum. It was not just his height; his shoulders and chest were all in proportion. He was a big man.

He would have been in his eighties at the time of our wedding but he still had a full head of thick wavy hair and his posture was that of a sentry at Buckingham Palace.

Despite his size, he was a very quiet man, with few words to say, so conversations were short. His dress was always working class Victorian, braces, Corduroy trousers, big boots, waist coat, and for our wedding, a pocket watch and chain.

Was his the reoccurring gene in our modern generation?

Matthew 1 v 1–17

Matthews Gospel starts with a detailed genealogy of the ancestors of Jesus.

It is the first gospel of the New Testament and a casual reading may cause the reader to wonder why it begins with a seemingly dull family tree. There may be a temptation to skip over it and get to where the action begins.

However, the genealogy is indispensable as it follows the birth of Christ back through the centuries to show that he is the legal descendent of King David's royal line.

This is essential in proving the fulfilment of the prophecies and the coming to pass of God's promise of the Messiah. The fulfilment that will take Jesus through his ministry and ultimately to death on the cross.

The genealogy is the interface between the Old and New Testaments.

Matthew begins his witness in the only way he could, by proving without doubt that Jesus is the Messiah, the son of God.

I am also blessed with a beautiful Great Granddaughter, Imogen, who is eighteen months old at the time I am writing this.

I am taller than she is – but for how long?

28

Believe it or Not

Mark 1 v 40–45   2 Kings 5 v 9–19

A couple of weeks ago I joined two or three hundred other people at four thirty in the afternoon, to descend on Derby Arena, a sports centre and music venue on the outskirts of Derby. Just to make it clear, we were not attending an illegal, 'Rave', and it was in compliance with COVID restrictions. We were all gradually making our way, in 2m intervals, towards having our COVID vaccinations.

As I was moving slowly but steadily towards the appointed chair, I began to realise that I actually knew very little about the substance that was shortly to be injected into my arm. I knew nothing about its chemical content, I knew nothing about how it will circulate around my body, and I didn't even know what it looked like.

So why did I believe that this act of vaccination could save my life and perhaps more importantly, save the lives of other people?

Many years ago, I was involved in MAYC (Methodist Association of Youth Clubs) and helped to organise Youth Weekends and workshops for young Christians. During some of the workshops we played a game which involved having one minute to explain to others why we passionately believed in something. This varied from football, and pop music, to fashion and food, but the most difficult one for our young people to explain, was why they believed in Jesus. After all everything we believe in Jesus is humanly impossible.

Jesus died on the cross, was buried, and on the third day he was raised from the dead, left the tomb and met with his disciples. He met them, not as a ghostly vision, but as flesh and blood. He ate and drank with the disciples. There is no wonder the young Christians had a problem in explaining their belief. We advised our young people to look at the evidence.

The Bible gives all the evidence we need, from different people at different times, and from different perspectives, but all giving the same message, that Jesus Christ is the Messiah, the Son of God and through belief in him we are saved.

The indisputable facts are what Jesus has done for each one of us on a personal level. Jesus has changed lives, given strength when we were weak, given hope when despair had taken hope away. Everything that Jesus has done for us is evidence that cannot be disputed.

In Mark's Gospel (Mark 1 v 40 to 45) we learn about a man with a dreaded skin disease who came to Jesus and begged him to make him clean, to heal him of the dreaded disease.

He was probably a Leper so would have been isolated from society so his visit to Jesus is surprising in itself.

We don't know if the man had met with Jesus before, or heard Jesus preaching, or just heard from other people about Jesus, but we know that this man believed that Jesus could and would heal him.

There was no doubt in his mind, he knew because he believed, and because he believed he was healed. The man believed that Jesus was the Son of God with the power to heal and the power to end the man's misery.

He approached Jesus with reverence, kneeling before him, he was desperate imploring Jesus to make him clean but he was humble by saying, 'If you are willing to heal me'. It was a personal request to Jesus and Jesus made a personal response.

Jesus reached out his hand – just think – the hand of God reaching out to answer a believer's prayer.

Jesus told the man not to publicize how he had been healed but to go directly to the Priest who was the only person who could declare the man healed. Unfortunately as so often is the case, the man was so excited over meeting with Jesus and being healed that he shouted from the rooftops.

Naaman in Kings (2 Kings 5 v 9 to 19) on the other hand was not so sure, and I'm not convinced that that he really believed that Elisha could heal him, but he thought it was worth a try. He was even less convinced when Elisha didn't even come out of his tent to see Naaman. He just sent a servant with a message, and it took considerable persuasion to get Naaman to bathe seven times in the Jorden. But when he did, he was healed and then he believed.

Unlike the man in Marks Gospel, Naaman needed the evidence before he believed.

Blessed are those who believe without seeing the evidence.

I can confirm that I had my vaccination and contrary to popular belief, my arm did not drop off, neither did I suffer from any of the multitude of side effects that other people had warned me about.

I just have to wait until April for the second instalment.

29

Full Steam Ahead

Daniel 7 v 1–14

The impact of the COVID restrictions has obviously had an effect on everything that we had become accustomed in our everyday lives. For me one of the frustrating issues has been the inability to indulge in my hobby of displaying my vintage tractors and classic car at the local rallies. In the past year every scheduled enthusiast's meeting has been cancelled and several of those in the near future have already been abandoned.

I know that in the big picture this minor inconvenience could be considered as insignificant, but never the less, it is still frustrating.

Although I enjoy taking my own vehicles, I also enjoy looking at the other exhibits, in particular the steam fairground engines. They are big, majestic, and powerful and yet when they are stationary they appear to be gentle, docile and almost timid, hiding all that power and energy behind highly polished brass and chrome and delicate artistic paintwork.

But my attraction and admiration of steam engines has not always been the case.

I can recall as a very young lad, holding onto my dad's hand in Bradford Foster Square Railway Station and I was screaming my head off in fear of a steam train. I can remember the occasion quire clearly but not the reason why we were there. It was not to go on a journey so possibly we were meeting someone, but whatever the reason I was definitely not happy.

In my eyes the steam engine was enormous and was belching out steam and smoke as if it was a giant dragonish monster. The air was filled with putrid sulphur smelling coal smoke and periodically an ear splitting hiss of pressurised steam would pierce my ear drums and then reverberate around the Victorian cathedral like station platform area.

Then, even worse was to come. The beast started to move, emitting thunderous explosions of smoke from the firebox, and high pressure steam into the pistons to force the wheels into motion. In that snapshot in time the world of that young lad had descended into a nightmare of smoke, steam, deafening sound and a fire breathing monster advancing towards him, and above all the turmoil my dad was shouting, ' Look son a steam train.'

This was no train; it was a dragon, sent to destroy us all but only I could see it.

Ironically, some seventy years later, my attraction to steam engines is the smoke, the steam, the smell, the sounds and the sheer presence of these giant monsters. They were a product of an age that revelled in extravagant engineering. Steam was the fulcrum of the industrial revolution in the Victorian era changing the direction of industry and travel not only in this country, but also across the mechanised world, only to be superseded by advanced technology and alternative fuels such as petrol, diesel and electricity.

Although now in retirement, the age of steam is not deceased and in the past ten years at least two brand new stream locomotives have been manufactured and can be seen touring the country (before COVID). Ever increasing miles (kilometres) of railway lines have been restored by enthusiasts in order to display these dragons of the past, but it has to be said that although my enthusiasm for steam is undoubtedly strong, in my mind it still takes me back to Bradford Foster Square Station's demonic dragon all those years ago.

Visions and dreams of multi-headed fearsome beasts and monsters are common in the Bible particularly in describing apocalyptic or cataclysmic events or prophecies and the book of Daniel is a good example of this kind of symbolism. It was written at a time when the Jews were suffering and living in constant fear of a pagan tyrant king and needed assurance that God had not forsaken them.

The Book of Daniel starts with his ability to interpret the King's (Nebuchadnezzar) dreams most significantly a dream of a man made of gold, silver and bronze but in Chapter 7 Daniel's role changes to be more prophetic. His vision describes four beasts rising from the sea and although the beasts relate back to the metal man earlier in Daniel 2, they all represent a terror that disturbs Daniel greatly.

It is a prophecy of five future Kingdoms;

The first is of a winged lion which represents the Babylonian Empire of Nebuchadnezzar.

The second is that of a stooping bear which represents the Persian Empire which will overcome the Babylonians.

The third is a winged four headed leopard which represents the Greek and Macedonian Empire.

The fourth is a fierce creature that was previously unknown, as strong as iron with the ability to crush anything underfoot. This represents the Roman Empire.

There is a fifth and final Kingdom which is that of the Messiah, one like the Son of Man descending with the clouds of Heaven (verse 13).

Although Daniel's vision depicted hard times and suffering to come, it also reassured and comforted both him and the Jewish nation, in that God's Kingdom through Jesus Christ will prevail over all evil.

My dad bought me a Tri-ang 00 gauge electric railway engine with four carriages and a coal tender. It ran on an oval shaped line and I bought myself a model water tank and a signal box.

Much better than the real thing.

30

Outstanding

1 Corinthians 1 v 2   Psalm 30 v 4

Recently, I received a telephone call from my eldest daughter. She was commuting to work and had heard a funny story on the radio and she seemed anxious to share it with me. The story was, why was the scarecrow recognised in the Queens Honours List? And the answer was, because he was outstanding in his field!

The strange sense of humour obviously runs in the family, but it did make me think how society does recognise the achievements of people who have made an outstanding contribution in their field or speciality over their lifetime.

The Queen's (or King's), honours list has for centuries recognised and honoured gallantry in battle, but has also recognised individuals who have given themselves for the benefit of others. Captain Sir Tom Moore is a perfect example of someone, who through his extraordinary efforts in raising millions of pounds for the NHS during the COVID crisis, has been honoured in this way. Sadly he passed away shortly before I produced this reflection.

Another source of recognition is by way of being awarded a Nobel Prize, which may be a little less familiar to many of us. These prizes are a product of a Swedish inventor and industrialist, Alfred Nobel, who on his death in 1895, bequeathed an allocation in his will to enable an annual prize to be awarded to, 'Those who during the preceding year, have conferred the greatest benefit to human kind'.

There are five separate categories for Nobel prizes, which are, 1) Chemistry, 2) Physics, 3) Physiology or Medicine, 4) Literature, and 5) Peace.

Nobel prizes differ insofar as they can be awarded to individuals, groups or even charitable organisations. An example is The International Committee of the Red Cross which has been the recipient of a Nobel Peace Prize on three separate occasions.

Although the scale and enormity of the Nobel Prize may be out of reach to most of us, and the selection process a bit secretive, some other recognition awards are widely publicised and enjoy the limelight of the press and other media. We have all witnessed the BAFTA and similar awards on our television screens, with all the glitter and glamour that we associate with the world of films, cinema and the arts. We have also witnessed the emotionally charged acceptance speeches of the recipients. In this case the industry itself is recognising exceptional skills, talents and personal efforts that have made an impact on the stage and screen.

Regardless of where in society an award or recognition has emanated it goes without saying that generally it is considered to be a great honour to be a recipient and to be aware that your work and achievements have been recognised and appreciated.

So, if it is a great honour to receive recognition in the secular world, how much more of an honour will it be to receive a similar recognition for contributing to the work of God through our Lord Jesus Christ?

In the eyes of the Roman Catholic Church a saint is a holy person who is known for his or her heroic sanctity. Saints are people from all walks of life who have dedicated their lives to the loving pursuit of God. Many, like St. Stephen were persecuted for their faith and ultimately forfeited their lives, while others like St. Mother Teresa worked tirelessly and devoted themselves to the service of the poor and disenfranchised.

The Bible contains many references to sainthood, and none are more prevalent than in Paul's letters to his churches. He emphasises that scripturally speaking the saints are the body of Christ, therefore all Christians can be considered to be, and called to be, saints.

1 Corinthians 1 v 2 states, 'To the church of God in Corinth, to those sanctified and holy', in other words to the saints in Corinth.

Similarly in Psalm 30 v 4 the Psalmist tells us to, 'Sing praises to the Lord O you his saints, and give thanks to his holy name.'

If we, as followers of Christ, are considered to be as saints called into his church, how honoured are we to be offered such an accolade and be privileged to do God's work in our world.

However, Paul also preaches that for him there is no accolade greater than to be recognised as an apostle of Christ and there is no reward greater than to see people brought to Jesus Christ through Paul's preaching. We do not carry out God's work for prizes, we do it for love of Jesus Christ and everything he did for us.

My dad had a great respect for the Monarchy and the honours list but he was shaken when pop stars, notably the Rolling Stones, received theirs. Dad's favourite comment was, 'If you gave them a pick and shovel they wouldn't know what to do with it.'

O for the generation gap.